# Counting Our Days

Roger Roberts

*Counting Our Days*
ISBN: Softcover 978-1-946478-73-3
Copyright © 2018 by Roger Daniel Roberts

All rights reserved. No part of this book may be reproduced or transmitted in any form or by any means, electronic or mechanical, including photocopying, recording, or by any information storage and retrieval system, without permission in writing from the publisher.

To order additional copies of this book, contact:
Parson's Porch Books
1-423-475-7308
www.parsonsporch.com

Parson's Porch Books is an imprint of **Parson's Porch & Book Publishers** in Cleveland, Tennessee, which has double focus. We focus on the needs of creative writers who need a professional publisher to get their work to market, **&** we also focus on the needs of others by sharing our profits with those who struggle in poverty to meet their basic needs of food, clothing, shelter and safety.

*Counting Our Days*

# Contents

Series Introduction ........................................................................... 7

The Greatest Test of Your Faith........................................................9
    Genesis 22: 1-14

When God's People Go Astray ....................................................... 15
    Exodus 32:1-14

The Presence of God ...................................................................... 22
    Exodus 33:12-23

Counting our Days.......................................................................... 29
    Psalm 90

Spiritual Depression: Its Causes and Cure .................................... 36
    Psalm 42

Trusting God .................................................................................. 43
    Psalm 139:1-18

The Money Choice ......................................................................... 50
    Matthew 6:19-24

Jesus' Invitation to Rest ................................................................. 57
    Matthew 11:25-30

Jesus' Call to Follow Him .............................................................. 63
    Mark 1:14-20

When Storms Come ....................................................................... 70
    Mark 4:35-41

Service: the Jesus Way to Greatness .............................................. 77
    Mark 10:35-45

Jesus Expects Fruit ......................................................................... 84
    Mark 11:12-14; 20-25

Waiting Orders ............................................................................... 90
    Luke 24:36-49

Jesus, the True Vine........................................................................ 96
    John 15:1-11

The Empty Tomb .................................................................. 102
    John 20:11-18

Doubting Thomas .................................................................. 108
    John 20:24-31

The Faith of a Young Girl ...................................................... 115
    Luke 1:26-45

Discipleship Is Following Jesus ............................................. 121
    Luke 9:57-62

An Advent Witness ................................................................ 128
    John 1:1-9

We Are People of the Cross .................................................. 135
    1 Corinthians 1:18-31

Run to Win! ........................................................................... 142
    1 Corinthians 9:19-27

How We Grieve ...................................................................... 148
    1 Thessalonians 4:13-18

Resurrection Children of God ............................................... 155
    1 John 2:28-3:3

# Series Introduction

Parson's Porch Books is delighted to present to you this series called *Sermons Matter*.

We believe that many of the best writers are pastors who take the role of preacher seriously. Week in, and week out, they exegete scripture, research material, write and deliver sermons in the context of the life of their particular congregation in their given community.

We further believe that sermons are extensions of Holy Scripture which need to be published beyond the manuscripts which are written for delivery each Sunday. Books serve as a vehicle for the sermon to continue to proclaim the Good News of the Morning to a broader audience.

We celebrate the wonderful occasion of the preaching event in Christian worship when the Pastor speaks, the People listen and the Work of the Church proceeds.

Take, Read, and Heed.

David Russell Tullock, M.Div., D.Min.
Publisher
Parson's Porch Books

# The Greatest Test of Your Faith

## Genesis 22: 1-14

*22 After these things God tested Abraham. He said to him, "Abraham!" And he said, "Here I am." 2 He said, "Take your son, your only son Isaac, whom you love, and go to the land of Moriah, and offer him there as a burnt offering on one of the mountains that I shall show you." 3 So Abraham rose early in the morning, saddled his donkey, and took two of his young men with him, and his son Isaac; he cut the wood for the burnt offering, and set out and went to the place in the distance that God had shown him. 4 On the third day Abraham looked up and saw the place far away. 5 Then Abraham said to his young men, "Stay here with the donkey; the boy and I will go over there; we will worship, and then we will come back to you." 6 Abraham took the wood of the burnt offering and laid it on his son Isaac, and he himself carried the fire and the knife. So, the two of them walked on together. 7 Isaac said to his father Abraham, "Father!" And he said, "Here I am, my son." He said, "The fire and the wood are here, but where being the lamb for a burnt offering?" 8 Abraham said, "God himself will provide the lamb for a burnt offering, my son." So, the two of them walked on together.*

*9 When they came to the place that God had shown him, Abraham built an altar there and laid the wood in order. He bound his son Isaac, and laid him on the altar, on top of the wood. 10 Then Abraham reached out his hand and took the knife to kill his son. 11 But the angel of the LORD called to him from heaven, and said, "Abraham, Abraham!" And he said, "Here I am." 12 He said, "Do not lay your hand on the boy or do anything to him; for now I know that you fear God, since you have not withheld your son, your only son, from me." 13 And Abraham looked up and saw a ram, caught in a thicket by its horns. Abraham went and took the ram and offered it up as a burnt offering instead of his son. 14 So Abraham called that place "The LORD will provide" as it is said to this day, "On the mount of the LORD it shall be provided."*

Most of my seminary classes began with a prayer, usually offered by the professor or a student. One student volunteered to offer the opening prayer, and earnestly implored, "Lord, help us as we take this test." "Test! What test? A panic-stricken student cried aloud, bringing the prayer to an abrupt halt.

The Christian life is a progression and maturing of our faith relationship with Christ, and along the way in our pilgrimage we face tests. Tests come in many forms, and are allowed by our loving God, not to distress us but to strengthen our faith and deepen our relationship with Christ. And unlike the student, we're not to be surprised when they come. Someday we'll face our greatest test of faith. Scripture says, "Consider it pure joy, my brothers, *whenever* you face trials of many kinds...." (Jas. 1:2). James doesn't say, *if* you face trials, but rather *whenever* you face them. He quickly adds that we can face trials with joy because God is at work through them to strengthen and deepen our love relationship with him. We don't need to dread our trials or even the greatest test of our faith. God's grace will always be sufficient.

It appears to me that Gethsemane was the hour when Jesus' human will was brought under his most severe testing. There, as he prayed agonizingly to the Father, he affirmed the cross as the will of God, and gained the peace of mind and strength of will to face his arrest and horrifying crucifixion. In the context of his Gethsemane prayer, Jesus warned Peter, James, and John to watch and pray in readiness for their hour of testing when their spirits might be willing but their flesh weak (Matt. 26:41).

Abraham had been tested before, and some tests he had passed, and with others he had faltered. Abraham's faith "chart" showed lapses of faith (Gen. 12:10; 16:1-4; 20:1-18); but his faith nevertheless did make upward progress, by the hand of God. But then, as we see, he came to his severest test, which was untimely, a rude interruption.

A severe test in my life and ministry was fifteen years ago, when crises at the church I was serving resulted in my resignation of a nineteen-year pastorate. All my ministry goals and plans were centered in that church, where I fully intended to retire after thirty of so years of service. The events that caught me totally by surprise were both unwelcome and untimely. It was at that point the greatest test of my life, forcing me to evaluate my calling and even my relationship with God. At the age of 57 I found myself asking, "Why now, Lord?"

During enjoying an international ministry in Brussels, Belgium, our lives were interrupted by my wife's Alzheimer's diagnosis, and the challenges inherent in that dreadful disease. Seeing my wife gradually die a slow and cruel death was a dreadful challenge and test of my Godward love and trust.

God tested Abraham with a demand (child sacrifice) that was a known practice in his time and surrounding culture. In our day, God would not ask us to literally sacrifice a child. Because of a fuller revelation in both the Old and the New Covenant we know that human sacrifice is abhorrent to God and is not his way of working. It was a unique test for Abraham, to sacrifice his "one and only son." Isaac was the fulfillment of God's promise to Abraham. Isaac's name means "laughter," and when he was born miraculously to 100-year-old Abraham and 90-year-old Sarah, they laughed in delight over the incredible fulfillment of the promise (Gen. 21:1-7).

When he commanded Abraham to sacrifice Isaac, God seemed to be against God (Chrysostom). To Abraham, the promise and commandment of God seemed self-contradictory, and in our time of greatest difficulty, it will seem the light of God's truth will be turned to darkness. In times of testing all we can do is simply trust in God's love. Faith teaches us that, whatever God allows to come our way, he's with us and will turn the random and senseless into something for our good (Rom. 8:28).

Perhaps you face the loss of a job, your marriage or your own health, ageing, or the approach of death, which seem to counter all your hopes and dreams. Life has been rendered absurd by these sudden turns. This story of Abraham's immediate obedience to this extreme, unthinkable command cannot help but move us to pity for Abraham. Imagine the heartbreak and turmoil in his spirit as he trudged up that mountain with his soon-to-be-sacrificed, long-hoped-for son. The demands of God's greatest test will seem unbearable, untimely, and unreasonable.

The great Christian thinker and writer, CS Lewis, was a long-time bachelor, until he met Joy Davidman, who became the love of his life. Shortly she was diagnosed with cancer, and the two were married when she lay in her hospital bed with only a short time to live. Lewis cried out against God for the untimeliness of Joy's death and of the seeming absence of God:

"Meanwhile, where is God? This is one of the most disquieting symptoms. When you are happy, so happy that you have no sense of needing Him…you will be—or so it feels—welcomed with open arms. But go to Him when your need is desperate, when all other help is vain, and what do you find? A door slammed in your face, and a sound of bolting and double bolting on the inside. After that, silence. You may as well turn away. The longer you wait, the more emphatic the silence will become." For the middle-aged CS Lewis, his test of faith seemed unbearable, just as for Abraham and Sarah, losing the delight of his life.

Perhaps the greatest heroes of the faith are not the miracle workers, but rather are the people who trust God even in the dark night of the soul, during times of contradictory circumstances when human reasoning would say, "Where is God?" Or, "…if God truly does exist, He would not allow such and such to happen, nor would He ask any of His children to do such an unreasonable thing."

By faith Abraham was willing to trust God, despite the untimely, the unreasonable, and the unbearable. Imagine how his heart broke when his son interrupted the silence, asking where the sacrifice was! Scripture tells us Abraham intended to obey, to sacrifice Isaac, trusting against all evidence that the Lord was able to raise him from the dead (Heb.11:17-19). But he didn't know for sure God would do that. In obedience, Abraham grabbed his confused and frightened son, and bound him to the cruel woodpile, and raised his knife to drive it into his heart.

No doubt, as Abraham proceeded up Mt Moriah with Isaac, Satan attacked his mind with thoughts such as, "What kind of God is this that you trust, who would ask you to kill your long-awaited son?" God's design is obvious only to him. Satan's design is for our destruction. And, as we look behind the scenes in Job, we note that in this fallen world, God's purposes of testing are often achieved by the initiative of Satan, who, in the words of Martin Luther, is God's devil. God may permit Satan to bring illness or human tragedy, but only according to God's ultimate will for our growth in faith and a deeper love relationship with him.

The Lord desires and is worthy of the devotion of our hearts and is jealous when we give him second place to anything or anyone else. The First Commandment is that we have no other gods before him (Ex. 20:3). Perhaps Isaac, the long-hoped-for promised son, had slipped into first place in Abraham's heart. As Bonhoeffer wrote, Jesus alone is to be the Mediator in our lives and nothing must come between him and us, not even our most beloved family members.

How subtly our love for Jesus and our devotion to him can be subordinated by what even appears to be noble care for our families! And the irony is, unless we love Jesus supremely, we'll never be able to love and care for our families as we ought. We don't do our children or anyone a favor when we turn them into idols. Even our religious work can become an idol that relegates our love for Jesus to a secondary place and presents a façade to others. Our worship becomes a mere routine and our religious work is done with hearts far from God (Matt. 15:1-9). God may ask you to put to death your ambition, goals, obsession and personal dreams and even loving plans for your family you have cherished in your heart. Someone wisely said that in the story of Abraham and Isaac, it wasn't Isaac who needed to die, but rather Abraham.

In the spring of 2003, in a time of deep soul searching and crying out to God, I prayed through our Scripture text for today. I told the Lord Jesus I was ready to take a knife to all my dreams and hopes as a pastor, believing that, if God desired me to continue in ministry he could raise a ministry from the dead. I asked Christ to let nothing come between me and him again, and to not let ministry be a substitute for loving and serving God.

The text in Hebrews 11 tells us that the faith of Abraham enabled him to reason with heavenly logic (the Greek word / verb in v. 19 gave rise to the English word "logic"), even though human logic failed him. Perhaps it's only when we stop relying on human logic that we begin to live and think by faith and begin to understand life from God's perspective.

Abraham, when he offered Isaac as a sacrifice, and obeyed God to the ultimate, saw God more clearly than before, and was made more mature in his faith. Tested faith includes a design from God, whose design is also to refine us. James, reflecting on Abraham's tested faith, says that because of Abraham's obedience he was made more mature in his faith (Jas. 2:22). Peter writes that trials come to us to test us, to refine our faith, which is as precious as gold refined in the fire. God is glorified as our faith is proved genuine (1 Pet. 1:7). In our trials Satan's design is to destroy or at least discourage us. But God is at work in our lives to refine us, deepen our love relationship, and make us more fitted for his purposes.

Life's greatest test may seem now nonsensical, but with heavenly logic we can see the hands of the loving Creator and heavenly Father at work to make us more usable to him, more bless-able now, and more reward-able in the eternal kingdom. God raised Abraham that day as a God-pleasing example of faith. Again, it wasn't Isaac who needed to die that day. It was old Abraham who needed to die on Mount Moriah, to be raised a new Abraham. He became that day what describes as a more loving, trusting, and beloved friend of God (Jas. 2:22), which is what God desires us to be (Matt. 22:36-40).

Abraham passed his greatest test. And so, may we.

# When God's People Go Astray

## Exodus 32:1-14

*When the people saw that Moses delayed to come down from the mountain, the people gathered around Aaron, and said to him, "Come, make gods for us, who shall go before us; as for this Moses, the man who brought us up out of the land of Egypt, we do not know what has become of him." ² Aaron said to them, "Take off the gold rings that are on the ears of your wives, your sons, and your daughters, and bring them to me." ³ So all the people took off the gold rings from their ears, and brought them to Aaron. ⁴ He took the gold from them, formed it in a mold, and cast an image of a calf; and they said, "These are your gods, O Israel, who brought you up out of the land of Egypt!" ⁵ When Aaron saw this, he built an altar before it; and Aaron made proclamation and said, "Tomorrow shall be a festival to the LORD." ⁶ They rose early the next day, and offered burnt offerings and brought sacrifices of well-being; and the people sat down to eat and drink, and rose up to revel.*

*⁷ The LORD said to Moses, "Go down at once! Your people, whom you brought up out of the land of Egypt, have acted perversely; ⁸ they have been quick to turn aside from the way that I commanded them; they have cast for themselves an image of a calf, and have worshiped it and sacrificed to it, and said, 'These are your gods, O Israel, who brought you up out of the land of Egypt!'" ⁹ The LORD said to Moses, "I have seen this people, how stiff-necked they are. ¹⁰ Now let me alone, so that my wrath may burn hot against them and I may consume them; and of you I will make a great nation."*

*¹¹ But Moses implored the LORD his God, and said, "O LORD, why does your wrath burn hot against your people, whom you brought out of the land of Egypt with great power and with a mighty hand? ¹² Why should the Egyptians say, 'It was with evil intent that he brought them out to kill them in the mountains, and to consume them from the face of the earth'? Turn from your fierce wrath; change your mind and do not bring disaster on your*

> *people. [13] Remember Abraham, Isaac, and Israel, your servants, how you swore to them by your own self, saying to them, 'I will multiply your descendants like the stars of heaven, and all this land that I have promised I will give to your descendants, and they shall inherit it forever.'" [14] And the* LORD *changed his mind about the disaster that he planned to bring on his people.*

Moses had been gone from the people during his audience with the Lord God for nearly six weeks, and the people became restless, and asked Moses' brother Aaron to construct an idol, a golden calf, in direct violation of the Second Commandment against idol construction and worship (20:4; 32:1).

Some preachers seem to enjoy preaching about sin and God's judgment. But I'm too much of a sinner myself to find such enjoyment and confidence that I'm above God's judgment. During my Baptist upbringing, the big sins, which I largely managed to avoid, were smoking, drinking, dancing and cussing. But I have realized that anything I think, say, feel or do that displeases God and harms myself or others is sin.

This account of the worship of the golden calf is not about what happens when pagans sin, but rather what happens when God's people sin. These sinning believers were delivered through the Sea, given the covenant and the Ten Commandments, and had just reaffirmed their commitment to obey and follow the Lord God (24:3).

This passage is a critically important one for us today as God's people. We too continue to engage in spiritual warfare and moral temptation because, if we're on our present earthly pilgrimage, we must resist the downward pull of the old sinful, fallen nature that Paul describes in Romans 7. The apostle also wrote to the Corinthians, giving them warnings from Israel's history, and specifically from this event at Mt Sinai. Paul refers to this event of idol worship resulting in sexual immorality, bringing God's judgment. He says that "These things happened to them to serve as an example, and they were written down to instruct us…. So, if you think you are standing, watch out that you do not fall" (1 Corinthians 10:11-12).

We need to carefully listen to what the Lord God is saying to us Baptists and Presbyterians about the subtle and sneaky prevalence of sin. Amazingly, so soon after their miraculous deliverance and God's dramatic revelation, their awe-inspired worship and vow of obedience, the people of God engaged in egregious rebellion. They stooped to the level of the false religion and immoral practices of the Egyptians. Once again, they demonstrated that it was easier to get the Israelites out of Egypt than to get Egypt out of the Israelites (Ryken).

In writing to the Galatians, Paul reminds us that we have a choice—to live by the Spirit a life that pleases God or to fall back into living according to the dictates of the sinful nature, and he gives a list of shameful behavior. I can manage to feel pretty good about myself regarding these shameful behavioral sins, but I can't dodge the more "respectful sins," such as strife, jealousy, anger and envy. I'm also guilty of the un-Christlike sins of selfishness, indifference toward the needy and inaction in the face of social injustice. When believers act or fail to act in these ways, whether in sordid or subtle ways, we're acting like pure pagans, who have never received eternal life and a new nature.

When Moses had been gone a while, the awareness of God's presence and goodness began to fade; and questions and doubts began to arise. Unless we turn to the Lord and remain steadfast in waiting upon and trusting in him, in the bad times as well as the good times, our questions and doubts can settle into unbelief. The impatience of the Israelites waiting for Moses for nearly six weeks gave way to doubt, which became unbelief. They became disappointed with God, who wasn't living up to their expectations and meeting their timetable.

Have you ever been disappointed with God? I have. And it's usually because I'm suffering from "spiritual amnesia" (Ryken). The Israelites forgot the God who saved them, who had done great things in Egypt, miracles in the land of Ham and awesome deeds by the Red Sea (Psalm 106:21f). And I forget what God has done for me in Christ, in his death and resurrection and in his gracious rescue from sin, death and hell. Once we forget the saving grace of God and our commitment to follow Jesus as Lord, we lose the focus of our lives. When we fail to worship, trust and love God, we'll find a substitute, an idol, which is a "god" of our own making.

We can construct a false god we sing about and pray to on Sundays, one who is not the living, loving, and holy God of the Scriptures. This will be the god of our own making, who suits our expectations and is eager to bless our every endeavor. When we listen to his preachers, we're entertained and comforted in our assurance that all he wants to do is make life more comfortable, and he'll otherwise leave us alone.

The Israelites who fell into idolatry began to live like the devil himself. They began to act like the pagan Egyptians. Those who claim to be God's children and whose lifestyle shows no difference from the fallen world, need to give themselves a reality check. The rebellious Israelites found a way to be "religious" and party, with a god that could condone their immoral behavior.

In my Baptist upbringing, we were good at avoiding certain "sins," at least the party-type sins. But God's desire is not to restrict our enjoyment of life. He's created us with certain appetites and desires for pleasure. God simply want us to gratify them in his way and time, in a way that maximizes pleasure and minimizes regret. Jesus knew how to have a good time, being accused of being "a glutton and a drunkard" (Matthew 11:19). Some overly strict prudes confuse sin with pleasure.

I heard of the daughter of a Presbyterian minister who, in his funeral eulogy, said that in his 90 years her father never committed a pleasure. That's not a life that pleases oneself or God, who created life to be enjoyed. Christians of all people should know how to party the right way! It's just important that we *invite God* to the party!

Sin is living apart from the will and presence of God. It's behavior that leaves God out of our lives. It's living as though God is absent or is making God less than he is. But God hates and judges sin, and not just sins of the flesh but of thought, speech and attitude. He hates sin because of what it does to us, bringing suffering, damage to the image of God and to our relationship with him and with others. God hates sin because of what it did to his Son, who suffered for us the consequences of and the just punishment for our sins. God hates sin because it disrupts our fellowship with him.

RC Sproul says we confuse God's justice and mercy, and we wonder why God's so upset about sin! Sproul notes that instead of singing the popular "Amazing Grace," we would prefer to sing the song, "Amazing Justice." We're amazed by God's justice and think we deserve his grace, by which we mean leniency. Referring to Jesus' recounting the falling of the tower in Siloam as a warning for all us sinners to repent (Luke 13:4f), Sproul continues: "Our lyrics tend to go like this:

> *Amazing Justice, cruel and sharp*
> *That wounds a saint like me:*
> *I'm so darn good it makes no sense—*
> *The tower fell on me"* (Sproul, 167).

God's judgment fell that day. Some people were spared, and others were destroyed. Moses' shattering the stone tablets seemed a ritual act that symbolized the breaking of God's covenant with the unrepentant. Amazingly, in response to Moses' intercession, "the Lord God changed his mind about the disaster he planned to bring on his people" (14). By grace through Moses' prayer, many were spared.

God revealed in Jesus hates sin just as much today. He's just as holy and righteous today as in his response to the sins of his people with the golden calf. God is the same yesterday, today and forever (Hebrews 13:8). But now God acts differently because a perfect sacrifice, a perfect Mediator has made atonement for our sin and has satisfied the wrath of God and his demands for justice. Because of what Christ has done, God, the just one, can act differently toward us. The good news of the story of Christ Jesus is that God's response to our sin can be different than it was with the Israelites with the golden calf. The judgment in Exodus 32 doesn't apply to us today. It isn't that God has changed, but rather that a Mediator has come. One who knew no sin became sin for us (2 Corinthians 5:21).

The episode of the golden calf has become good news for us because of the vital difference the cross of Christ and the empty tomb have made for us (1 Peter 3:18). We have, just like the people of the Old Covenant, failed to live up to the righteous requirements of the law and have failed to live a life that pleases God and that receives the full measure of his blessing. Like these Israelites, we've been caught in the act of our sin, and deserve God's judgment; but like Moses stood between these sinful Israelites and turned away God's judgment, so Christ, taking our guilt upon himself as he suffered and died on the cross, gives forgiveness and peace with God to those who turn to him in faith and repentance.

The golden calf shows us how *not* to live. Disobedience and idolatry, living for someone or something other than God leads to self-destructive and Christ-dishonoring behavior, which is sin. For a child of God, living in rebellion is a dangerous life. "It is a dreadful thing to fall into the hands of the living God" (Hebrews 10:31). God loves us so much, he'll take sometimes drastic and painful measures to bring us back into his love and fellowship. A life outside of God's will that brings dishonor to his name is mortally dangerous, as we read from Paul (1 Corinthians 5:4f) and John (1 John 5:16). Paul says that God's judgment on the rebellious Israelites is a serious example and warning to rebellious believers (1 Corinthians 10:11).

God hates sin, but he loves us and yearns for us to return to him. Another great picture we have of the heart of God is that of the father of the Prodigal Son in Luke 15:11-32). This is the way God acts toward us today. Although the rebellious son went his own way toward self-destruction the father always yearned for him to return home. God yearns to forgive, restore and bless you with his love, eternal life, joy and fellowship. He wants you to have joy and peace in your life.

God loves us so much he'll take severe measures to bring us back into his love. We need to take inventory of our walk with Christ in the light of the golden calf, and as John admonished, be sure we are keeping our lives free from idols (1 John 5:21), that nothing and no one is more important in our lives than Christ and that he is

Lord over everything we are and all that we have. I pray that we'll respond to God's gracious warning about what happens when we sin, and that we'll seek his mercy and grace. He yearns for us to come home! He loves us sinners unconditionally.

# The Presence of God

## Exodus 33:12-23

*¹²Moses said to the* LORD, *"See, you have said to me, 'Bring up this people'; but you have not let me know whom you will send with me. Yet you have said, 'I know you by name, and you have also found favor in my sight.' ¹³ Now if I have found favor in your sight, show me your ways, so that I may know you and find favor in your sight. Consider too that this nation is your people."¹⁴ He said, "My presence will go with you, and I will give you rest." ¹⁵ And he said to him, "If your presence will not go, do not carry us up from here. ¹⁶ For how shall it be known that I have found favor in your sight, I and your people, unless you go with us? In this way, we shall be distinct, I and your people, from every people on the face of the earth."*

*¹⁷ The* LORD *said to Moses, "I will do the very thing that you have asked; for you have found favor in my sight, and I know you by name." ¹⁸ Moses said, "Show me your glory, I pray." ¹⁹ And he said, "I will make all my goodness pass before you, and will proclaim before you the name, 'The* LORD*'; and I will be gracious to whom I will be gracious, and will show mercy on whom I will show mercy. ²⁰ But," he said, "you cannot see my face; for no one shall see me and live." ²¹ And the* LORD *continued, "See, there is a place by me where you shall stand on the rock; ²² and while my glory passes by I will put you in a cleft of the rock, and I will cover you with my hand until I have passed by; ²³ then I will take away my hand, and you shall see my back; but my face shall not be seen."*

There's just no substitute for presence, especially with someone you love and who loves you. Communication technology, like email, long-distance telephone, and Skype and now Facetime, were very important during our years in Belgium when separated from family and friends by 5,000 or so miles. But reuniting in person is so much better!

Talk with young and even older adults who are struggling with security and self-esteem issues and many will express their resentment or sorrow over the fact that their parents simply were not there for them during their critically formative years. Ambitious and/or wealthy parents who substituted giving expensive toys and other gifts to their children, like smart phones, are nevertheless resented because they were unwilling to give their involvement. The same is true with children from broken or dysfunctional homes, with an absent father or negligent parent.

We're made for personal relationships and depend on personal connections for mental and emotional health. Prisoners in solitary confinement are candidates for insanity. God created us for relationship with him and each other, and no one can be healthy or complete apart from knowing God in a personal way. God called the people of Israel into a personal relationship with himself, to know him and to experience the fellowship of his presence and made a covenant with Abraham to have a people who would be distinctly his and who would be his dwelling place (Gen. 12:1f; 15:1ff).

Those who were graciously spared God's judgment for the golden calf suddenly realized there's no substitute for his presence. God called them and brought them out of Egypt, across the sea and to Mt Sinai, where God gave them his covenant law and they made their covenant promises to him. But now God's presence was at risk.

When the Lord God said that he would not go with them on the rest of their journey to the Promised Land the Israelites were distressed (2f). This wasn't merely a setback; it meant the end of the road. The Lord God himself had accompanied, protected and provided for the Israelites, and the thought of having to depend on an ordinary angel was frightening, knowing what they were up against. They depended on the Lord God *for deliverance*.

We too need to come to that crucial realization. Apart from the presence of God we're hopelessly lost. Even for mortal life, we depend on the presence of God and his goodness. Jesus refers to this general grace and goodness when he says how the Father in heaven causes his sun to rise on the evil and the good and sends rain on the righteous and unrighteous (Matt. 5:45). Although they wouldn't admit it, militant atheists like Richard Dawkins depend on God's general grace.

Although we know there is immeasurable suffering and gross injustice in this fallen world, we also should recognize that the presence of God mitigates suffering and holds many disasters and untold tragedies in check. Everyone, regardless of unbelief or immoral conduct, knows something of this general grace and longsuffering of a God who doesn't want anyone to perish, but desires everyone to come to repentance (2 Pet. 3:9). Hell is the only place where God is not to some degree present, which is why it's a place of absolute hopelessness and unmitigated suffering and darkness. Those who finally reject God's deliverance through Christ and spurn his saving grace will have chosen hell as the only option to his presence.

Like the Israelites we too depend on God's presence for our guidance and daily grace. He alone is omniscient and, as their psalmist would later put to poetry and music, is our faithful and good Shepherd (Ps. 23:1; 28:9; 78:71). Because the Lord God is omnipotent, omniscient, faithful and loving, we can trust him to guide us in the way we should go. The Israelites had seen God miraculously and faithfully provide water and manna and deliverance from their enemies, and the prospects of moving forward without him were frightening.

What a blessed relief it must have been when the Lord God assured Moses that he would in fact go with them (14)! The Lord promised that he would give them his rest, which is more literally translated "roost." His presence would give them a place to roost, like a bird and her chicks, under his wings of protection and provision. Wherever we are, because God is with us, he enables us to "roost," "to settle down for rest." His presence can give us a sense of peace and settled-ness even in the most unsettling of circumstances.

A personal relationship with God is the distinctive mark of his people. Moses' appeal for the Lord's presence to distinguish his people is all important. Some are happy to have the Lord's presence simply to help them reach their goal of the Promised Land, but otherwise leave them alone. A lot of so-called Christians want to "go to heaven when they die" and are more than happy for God to help them make a good living, keep their kids out of trouble, and help them survive accidents and illnesses. But beyond his general grace and goodness and benefits, they would prefer that God not interfere with their lives.

Just as for the Israelites, the presence of God isn't always comfortable. As Charles Spurgeon said, "God never permits his people to sin successfully." If we truly belong to God, he'll make his errant children miserable until we come back to him for restored fellowship. God's presence comforts the disturbed but disturbs the comfortable. As Paul Scherer says, "no place on earth can be called 'safe in the arms of Jesus,'" and "None of my Sunday school teachers ever told me how dangerous a place that was!"

God allows experiences, including difficulties and suffering, to draw us closer to his love, deeper into his joy, and to produce more of his character in us (Rom. 5:1-5; Jas. 1:2-4). Honest relationships require open communication, even when it's uncomfortable.

With all our electronic communications gadgetry, many seem to ignore live interaction and personal communion, like couples and even entire families, sitting at a restaurant table, all absorbed with their own smart phones and basically ignoring each other. Strong relationships demand communication, even when it's uncomfortable; maybe especially when it's uncomfortable.

Moses desperately needed God's presence, but he also desired an even greater intimacy with him. Moses wanted to see God's full glory, which was not possible. Moses' request came about 1450 years too soon. The Apostle John writes that the Word, Christ, "became flesh and lived among us, and we have seen his glory, the glory as of a father's only son, full of grace and truth" (Jn. 1:14). The amazing truth is, that because Christ came to be "God with us" (Matt. 1:23) we can see more than Moses saw. In fact, "the Christian child, who looks upon the 'glory of God in the face of

Jesus Christ,' has a vision which outshines the flashing radiance that shone round Moses" (Maclaren).

We've seen "the light of the knowledge of the glory of God in the face of Jesus Christ" (2 Cor. 4:6). Moses' face shone after he had been in the tent of meeting with God, but Paul says that each one of God's people in the New Covenant "reflect the Lord's glory" and are being transformed into the likeness of Christ "with ever-increasing glory" by the Holy Spirit (2 Cor. 3:18). By faith we're more blessed that those who saw Jesus in his physical presence, Jesus says when we see him by faith (Jn. 20:29). We see the glory of God as we see Jesus on the cross and risen from the grave and trust and follow him as our risen Lord and Savior.

The Lord told Moses he would be allowed to see his goodness and hear his name, which revealed his character (19). We can see the perfect character of Jesus as the divine Son of God, who said, "Anyone who has seen me has seen the Father" (Jn. 14:9). When we see the person and character of Christ in Jesus, revealed to us in Scripture and by the Holy Spirit, we see God's saving glory. The Lord told Moses he would be hidden by his hand in the cleft of a rock when his glory passed by, then Moses could see the glory from behind but would not be allowed to see God's face, the fullness of his glory (21ff). What we can see also at times is the glory from behind, as God lets us see what his presence has done.

The greatest disclosure of past glory is that of the cross and the empty tomb, what God has done for our deliverance. We can also see his glory through the 2,000 years of church history and what he has done for us in recent years. Sometimes in personal worship but also in our corporate worship, only after it's all said and done do I see traces of God's glory, the work he's done. There are times I have left a hospital room after a time of glorious prayer with a dying saint, and have thought to myself the words of Jacob at Bethel:

"'Surely the Lord is in this place, and I was not aware of it.' He was afraid and said, 'How awesome is this place! This is none other than the house of God; this is the gate of heaven'" (Genesis 28:16f).

Like Moses, our desire should be, not for his material blessings, but for God himself. Throughout our text we find the verb "to know," and it's a word of personal knowledge and experience. The Apostle Paul also had this deep desire to know God in a deeper way, and he realized that the pathway to the deepest, most intimate knowledge of Christ was not just to experience the power of his resurrection but also "the fellowship of sharing in his sufferings, becoming like him in his death" (Phil. 3:10). There can be no true intimacy with Christ apart from the way of the cross of self-denial and suffering.

Martin Luther King, Jr. was a rising star in a prominent pastorate in Atlanta when challenged to lead in the civil rights movement, which suddenly brought death threats against him and his young family. One night when sleep failed him as fearful thoughts flooded his mind, alone at his kitchen table, the words of an old gospel song gave him comfort and courage:

"No never alone, no never alone. He promised never to leave me, never to leave me alone." Because the Lord promised to be with him, young King feared to disobey God more than he feared the dangers that lay before him.

God's people depend on and desire his presence. Have you discovered the joy as well as the dangerous challenge of the presence of the Lord? You can't Skype, Facetime him or even direct dial him long distance on your phone or send him an email. He's available only in person, in his awesome, sin-consuming presence that makes an immediate and everlasting change in your life.

His presence means he guides you and delivers you through life's dangers and provides all your needs, but not all your wants. But you can be confident that his way is best, and that he is always with us, even when it doesn't look it or feel like it.

The psalmist said: "Seek the Lord and his strength; seek his presence continually" (Psalm 105:4). The Lord Jesus has promised to be with me always, so I need affirm that the Lord and his strength are with me, reminding myself that God is with me, whether I realize it or not, whether I feel spiritually full or empty

(Matt. 28:20). He seeks me to strengthen me. He's with me always because he promised. He's here. He's with me and he's with you, always.

# Counting our Days

## Psalm 90

Lord, you have been our dwelling place
  in all generations.
2 Before the mountains were brought forth,
  or ever you had formed the earth and the world,
  from everlasting to everlasting you are God.

3 You turn us back to dust,
  and say, "Turn back, you mortals."
4 For a thousand years in your sight
  are like yesterday when it is past,
  or like a watch in the night.

5 You sweep them away; they are like a dream,
  like grass that is renewed in the morning;
6 in the morning it flourishes and is renewed;
  in the evening it fades and withers.

7 For we are consumed by your anger;
  by your wrath we are overwhelmed.
8 You have set our iniquities before you,
  our secret sins in the light of your countenance.

9 For all our days pass away under your wrath;
  our years come to an end like a sigh.
10 The days of our life are seventy years,
  or perhaps eighty, if we are strong;
even then their span is only toil and trouble;
  they are soon gone, and we fly away.

11 Who considers the power of your anger?
  Your wrath is as great as the fear that is due you.
12 So teach us to count our days
  that we may gain a wise heart.

> 13 Turn, O Lord! How long?
>   Have compassion on your servants!
> 14 Satisfy us in the morning with your steadfast love,
>   so that we may rejoice and be glad all our days.
> 15 Make us glad as many days as you have afflicted us,
>   and as many years as we have seen evil.
> 16 Let your work be manifest to your servants,
>   and your glorious power to their children.
> 17 Let the favor of the Lord our God be upon us,
>   and prosper for us the work of our hands—
>   O prosper the work of our hands!

Years ago, I read a book on time management that gave one of the most profound statements I had ever read on the subject. The author said that time management is a misnomer. We cannot manage time. Time is inexorable and is something created by our eternal God. Time is measured for us by the rotation of the earth and its orbit around the sun. Give or take a few seconds, whether the earth might wobble on its axis, time is the same every year. This we know by the precise measurement of atomic clocks. And so, we cannot manage time; we can only manage ourselves and how we live within time, as it rolls relentlessly along (Leas).

Most of us have electronic gadgets that promised to help us manage our use of time. Technology has made a significant contribution to our work and communication efficiency, but I'm not sure how much time it saves us. Without good time management principles and self-discipline, our time saving devices can just rob us of time.

Our psalm uses an expression that will help us get a grip on the matter of managing life in respect to time. Moses prays:

> "So, teach us to count our days
>   that we may gain a wise heart."

Moses prays that his life might have maximum significance. He doesn't want to end his life having been victimized by squandered time. Eternal God created time and space in all its complexity and vastness. This psalm contrasts the immortality of God with the transient nature of human life. Since the fall of Adam and Eve in the Garden of Eden, mankind is under the sentence of mortality, a condition we share with the beasts (Ps. 49:12). God desires our life with him forever, but the result of rebellion against God's intention was death—moral, spiritual and mortal death. "The wages of sin are death," Paul writes (Rom. 6:23), and mortal death is the last enemy mankind, including followers of Christ, will face (1 Cor. 15:26).

We are given the gift of mortal life, and for many of us, this earthly life receives many of the blessings of God. While we have these days upon the earth, we face the choice of how we should live them. The psalm reminds us that "time flies," that our mortal lives are brief indeed. "A watch in the night" (4b) was the ancient's shortest measure of time" (Weisur).

Four years ago, I attended a reunion of my high school graduating class in Columbus, Ohio. I hadn't seen most of these people in 50 years, when we were 18-year-old high school graduates. I think we were all a bit stunned to see what time had done to each other, as we were rudely confronted with the cruelty of the aging process. Possibly an underlying question running through a lot of minds, believers and unbelievers alike was "What did you do with your life?"

The psalmist expresses a lament over the trouble and sorrow that often accompanies our brief mortal life (7-11).

A few years ago, Kyle and I took his mother to the UW emergency department. While we waited with her to be taken to a room, we noted the various people brought for emergency treatment, victims of accidents, or weakened condition from age or illness. We said to each other, "Life looks very fragile and brief in this setting, doesn't it?"

Our psalm laments the brevity of mortal life, citing what was then the average life span of 70 to 80 years. Typically for young people, the thought is "I'll live forever!" At least this was true for me. But whatever age we might reach, we live under the scrutiny of a holy

God, who will hold us accountable for our use of our lives. Life passes quickly by and "we fly away" (10). Everyone is given mortal life and with that gift comes a responsibility. Jesus spoke of degrees of responsibility based on opportunity. As he concluded a parable contrasting faithful and unfaithful servants, Jesus said,

"From everyone who has been given much, much will be demanded; and from the one who has been entrusted with much, much more will be asked" (Lk. 12:48).

Apart from a personal relationship with God, the highest purpose and the greatest joys in life are forfeited. Life is squandered simply by spending life on lesser and temporal things. I'm not saying that for unbelievers and those who give themselves to lesser things have made no contribution to society, nor have they experienced nothing of happiness and satisfaction. Indeed, God blesses and uses various contributions for the public good, regardless of the personal beliefs of those who make those contributions.

In Jesus' parable of the rich fool, God called the rich man a fool because, even though he was a shrewd businessman, he squandered his life on the selfish pursuit of the material, oblivious to the eternal. Jesus said anyone is foolish and faces the ultimate loss of all things who does not seek to be rich towards God (Lk. 12:13-21). Did you ever see this bumper sticker? "The one who dies with the most toys wins." Some, even so-called Christians, squander their lives in pursuit of material gain, which the Bible says is absolute folly.

We're called to live our lives as stewards of God-given opportunities. Unless we live in prayerful and loving fellowship with God, seeking to know him better and follow his will, we as followers of Jesus run the risk of squandering our opportunities to deepen our relationship with him. The Scriptures speak of the judgment seat of Christ before which we all must stand and give an account of how well we have seized and used the opportunities God has given us, to know him better, to love and enjoy him deeply and serve him faithfully. We can squander God-given time and opportunities and expect to face the opprobrium of God's judgment seat (2 Cor. 5:10; Rom. 14:10).

The iniquities that God has set before his view may not be just the overt sins of our lives; not just wrongs committed, said and thought. But God is also aware of those opportunities he has given us to know and show his love each day, to share our faith in a caring, meaningful way and to seek to encourage the Body of Christ. He has placed us all in our sphere of influence, including our neighborhoods. The family around your dinner table, the neighbors on your street, your fellow employees and students, are opportunities for us. To neglect to make a difference is to squander those God-given opportunities. And what God is expecting are not always and maybe not even mostly the big things we do, the large ministry projects, but how I am thinking and acting like Jesus, receiving and sharing his love each day. Am I daily becoming more like Jesus and allowing him to live his life of loving service through me and as me?

The first of the psalm is hymn and lament, but now the man of God, Moses, turns to prayer, that his remaining days will be invested wisely (12-17). He prays that the eternal God will teach us mortals how to live wisely within time. We're immortal souls living mortal lives, which isn't an easy fit.

CS Lewis noted how *"we are so little reconciled to time that we are even astonished at it. 'How he's grown!' we exclaim, 'How time flies!' as though the universal form of our experience were again and again a novelty. It is as strange as if a fish were repeatedly surprised at the wetness of water. And that would be strange indeed,"* notes Lewis, *"unless of course the fish were destined to become, one day, a land animal."*

God has made us mortals as the crown of his creation and as such we have this witness of eternity, this yearning for immortality. Our new, regenerate heart of wisdom enables us to fear and love God and to share his perspective on life, time and eternity. We have a sense of the brevity and the frailty of mortal life and realize that we are to live our days of this mortal life before God, with a sense of accountability to him as his servants, his stewards, and his children. The Apostle Paul writes that we must "be steadfast, immovable, always excelling in the work of the Lord, because you know that in the Lord your labor is not in vain" (1 Cor. 15:58).

With this God-given new heart of wisdom, we can invest our days wisely living joyfully and fruitfully. Moses understands the importance of joy in his life and labor (14). When we invest our lives wisely, the result is joy. Moses remembers the days that the Israelites were afflicted in Egypt and in their wilderness wanderings, when they experienced God's discipline that always followed periods of their rebellion. He prays that the Lord will now make them glad for as many days as he afflicted them (15). As Old Testament scholar Derek Kidner writes, this modest prayer is "outrun" by the Apostle Paul:

> *"For this slight momentary affliction is preparing us for an eternal weight of glory beyond all measure."* (2 Cor. 4:17).

Even in life's greatest difficulties and challenges, and perhaps particularly during these tough times, God is at work shaping us into the restored image of Christ, drawing us deeper into his true joy, and showing more of his glory to the world around us. And all of this will result in our greater glory in the new heaven and earth.

The prayer ends with a petition that the favor of the Lord our God will rest upon us and that he will establish the work of our hands for us (17). We all would like to think that our life's work and the living of our days have significance and will not end with our funeral. And the promise of the Lord is that what we do for him will endure the judgment and will be an everlasting memorial and glory to God (1 Cor. 3:10-15).

You and I must make tough choices with our time, shuffling schedules to give the right priorities: worship, spiritual formation, kingdom service, which begins first with our own families. He will enable us to attend to our real priorities.

The Great Awakening evangelist and founder of the Methodists, John Wesley, said simply and profoundly, "Our people die well." No doubt he meant they lived well and, in such hope, that they gladly faced death, which they were confident would usher them into the presence of Christ.

*Counting Our Days*

Two of our dear, long-time and faithful church members who both seem near the end of their mortal lives, I'm confident will also die well. That's because they have become sweet, godly people of a strong and blessed hope. Instead of fearing death or regretting their lives, they are praying that the Lord will release them from their constant pain and welcome them into his arms in Paradise.

As you know, Mary has lost almost all her speaking capacity, and must communicate mostly with her phone keypad. When I asked her if she was looking forward to being with Jesus, she raised her little hand and gave a "thumbs up." She has no regrets and has a glorious eternity ahead, because she's lived well, having become a sweet and Christlike child of God.

Lord, teach me to live wisely and so count my days.

# Spiritual Depression: Its Causes and Cure

## Psalm 42

*As a deer longs for flowing streams,
 so my soul longs for you, O God.
2 My soul thirsts for God,
 for the living God.
When shall I come and behold
 the face of God?
3 My tears have been my food
 day and night,
while people say to me continually,
 "Where is your God?"*

*4 These things I remember,
 as I pour out my soul:
how I went with the throng,
 and led them in procession to the house of God,
with glad shouts and songs of thanksgiving,
 a multitude keeping festival.
5 Why are you cast down, O my soul,
 and why are you disquieted within me?
Hope in God; for I shall again praise him,
 my help 6 and my God.*

*My soul is cast down within me;
 therefore I remember you
from the land of Jordan and of Hermon,
 from Mount Mizar.
7 Deep calls to deep
 at the thunder of your cataracts;
all your waves and your billows
 have gone over me.
8 By day the Lord commands his steadfast love,
 and at night his song is with me,
 a prayer to the God of my life.*

*9 I say to God, my rock,*
  *"Why have you forgotten me?*
*Why must I walk about mournfully*
  *because the enemy oppresses me?"*
*10 As with a deadly wound in my body,*
  *my adversaries taunt me,*
*while they say to me continually,*
  *"Where is your God?"*

*11 Why are you cast down, O my soul,*
  *and why are you disquieted within me?*
*Hope in God; for I shall again praise him,*
  *my help and my God.*

While most of the Scriptures speak *to* us, many of the Psalms speak *for* us, expressing our thoughts, prayers and emotions, including negative ones. The Psalms give their blessings to honest lamentations, expressing for us our emotions of fear, anger and anxiety, and our thoughts of guilt, doubt and bewilderment. One of the reasons that the Psalms are so popular and beloved is the fact that they resonate with so many human emotions and assure us that God welcomes our honest expressions of doubt, anger and, as with our passage today, our spiritual depression.

Likely, if all the statistics I've been reading are anywhere close to accurate, when I speak about spiritual and emotional depression I'm speaking to a condition that affects about a fourth of this congregation at this present time. Emotional depression is known by psychologists as "the common cold" among psychological disorders and that "Christians, though they find hope in their relationship with Jesus, are not exempt from struggling with this painful and serious problem," which afflicts between thirty to forty million Americans (A Kreger). Josh McDowell lists as possible causes of depression: biological factors (PMS, postpartum, glandular disorders, etc.); helplessness to remedy an intolerable situation (a difficult marriage, loss of a loved one); parental rejection; abuse; negative thinking; stress; anger, and guilt. No one is exempt from spiritual depression, not even your pastor! So, I'll be the last person to condemn you for being spiritually depressed. Although we're liable to suffer depression, we're not condemned to remain there. God comes to us in his word today to show us the way to overcome spiritual depression. The picture in our text is of a desperate deer, seeking water for his thirst. The psalmist realizes that he suffers from a drought of his soul and the only cure for his spiritual depression is found in God.

At Jacob's Well, Jesus met a woman who is representative of the human condition. She had tried to slake her God-given thirst at a dry well of futility—through finding the perfect relationship with a man. And man, after man (for a total of six) had disappointed her and left her with an unquenched thirst, a dry soul. And so, Jesus told her about a spring of water that would be the source of eternal and soul-satisfying life. Through a relationship with God she would find that true and everlasting satisfaction for which she had unwittingly longed (Jn. 4:13f).

Spiritual depression is the natural condition of any and every person who's in need of the source of living water, a soul-satisfying relationship with the living God. The unbeliever may be unaware of that thirst and finds temporary relief in physical pleasures and personal pursuits and other efforts at self-fulfillment. During his spiritual depression the psalmist, whom we can assume knew God as the only source of true satisfaction, cried out in lamentation over his thirst for God. He expressed his longing for the satisfaction he had found but somehow how lost during his pilgrimage of faith.

We don't know the circumstances of the psalmist, but there seems to be a progression in his misery. First, the psalmist senses that the God he had known and had called upon in the past was now far away. Literally, he was far away from the temple in Jerusalem, which was thought to be the focal point of the presence of God. And spiritual depression is likely to come upon us when God seems far away. We find ourselves longing for "the good old days," maybe when we first came to the "temple," when we were joyful, young believers.

At first, it seemed that God was answering one prayer after another. And since then, we have experienced, disappointments in unanswered prayer and, as Larry Crabb says, "shattered dreams," which are likely to come to every child of God. In fact, Crabb, a counselor and psychologist, says that "Answered prayer seems to be more frequently reported among younger Christians." New Christians need the assurance of God's presence, Crabb explains, and the more we mature the more God allows testing to come to our lives to wean us away from dependence on a "pleasant life." "Live long enough, Crabb writes, "and important dreams will shatter."

Some often believe that once they become a follower of Christ, they've found "the good life," and that God is committed to making life more pleasant and successful. But that's not what Jesus promised as "abundant life." The abundant life is one filled with spiritual blessings, the kind that make us more like Christ and that enables us to live a cruciform life of hope, not blessings that make this mortal life more comfortable. God loves us so much that he is willing to allow our earthly dreams, even good ones that we thought would honor God, to be shattered, so that we might seek him instead of pursuing our personal dreams.

Perhaps you're experiencing circumstances that have made God seem far away. Maybe you prayed for something or someone that ended in disappointment. Maybe your prayers for your marriage, your health or your rebellious child have gone unanswered. It seems that God is far away, that the encouragement and support you used to receive from your personal prayer and corporate worship are no longer there. Possibly, if you're like me, you suffer from not thinking you're good enough. You don't measure up to other's and even your own expectations of yourself, still trying to please others. And so, your soul is downcast.

In the second stanza (42:6-10), the psalmist expresses an even deeper depression when he thinks that God has forgotten him. The irony is, he remembered God (42:4,6), but God forgot him (42:9). At first, he suffered thirst of soul (42:1f): he was desperately dry, but now he is drowning in trouble, overwhelmed by life's waterfalls and waves (42:7).

The psalmist was a believer and, if given a theological or biblical exam he would have answered that he believed in God and in his love, power and sovereignty. But because of his circumstances, perhaps more shattered dreams, it certainly feels like God has forgotten him. Perhaps now the psalmist has begun to be overwhelmed by illness, pain and adversity. When pain begins to wreak its havoc upon our emotions, it seems that God has simply forgotten us.

God loves us too much to always come to our rescue and answer every prayer and meet every felt need in our lives. He practices a "severe mercy" and sometimes a tough love, allowing us to go through trials. His purpose perhaps is to wean us from dependence on lesser things and draw us away from the distractions of our personal pursuits, pleasures and self-directed agendas. We cry to him out of our illness for healing or for other help and he seems to have forgotten we're his children.

We may feel abandoned, but the Son was abandoned by the Father during that eternity of three hours of darkness when he cried from the cross, "My God, my God, why have you forsaken me?" (Matt. 27:46). Jesus was forsaken on the cross. The eternal Son was for the first moment in all eternity separated from the love of the Father to guarantee that we'll never be separated from the Father's love. When we, during our times of depression over our shattered dreams, are tempted to think we are forsaken, we need to look to the cross.

God loves us so much he'll take us all the way to the "brink" if that's what it takes for us to abandon ourselves to him, to relinquish our hold on lesser desires that keep us from loving God fully. We'll not be forsaken, but we'll likely feel forsaken, which may be the "fellowship of sharing in his (Christ's) sufferings," which Paul desired as a necessary part of knowing Christ fully (Phil. 3:10).

Just when we think we can take no more, that the waves are just about to drown us, God will deliver us, just as he delivered his Son from his suffering and death on the cross to his glorious resurrection. The psalmist cried out for God to vindicate him and rescue him from the wicked (43:1). As was true for him, our deliverance is assured through the victory of Christ in our behalf. We're more than conquerors through him (Rom. 8:37), and our conquest is over the real enemy—Satan. Others that oppose us and those who despise us are not the real enemy but are instead simply dupes of the devil.

As we note in these three refrains, the psalmist seems to stop himself in his tracks and confronts himself with this repeated question: "Why are you downcast, O my soul? Why so disturbed within me?" It's possible to get "bogged down" in our spiritual depression, with obsessive introspection, which can lead to morbidity. Instead of introspection we need, like the psalmist, to engage in a healthy self-examination. The psalmist preaches to himself (Lloyd-Jones). And likewise, we too must say to our soul, "Why are you downcast"?

It's important to know our physical condition since depression can relate to our health. There are times when we may well need to see a doctor or professional counselor, if we think our depression may be physical or psychosomatically related and beyond our coping power. Likewise, more children, young people and adults than ever before, Christians included, suffer from childhood traumas associated with neglect or abuse. There may also be struggles with one's sexual identity and other problems that might require the care and counsel of a professional. We also need to be aware of personality types and characteristic predisposition to melancholia and then adjust our lives accordingly. Some simply need more support from professionals, friends and a strong Christian social network.

There are some common-sense things we can do to counter proclivity to depression, such as proper sleep and rest, healthy diet and adequate exercise and enjoyable recreation and friendships. Of course, maintaining the spiritual disciplines of worship, Scripture reading and meditation, fellowship and service in the Body of Christ (which may necessitate reconciliation with alienated brothers and sisters in Christ) are all antidotes to spiritual depression.

But likely, we usually need to get alone with God. "Put you hope in God," the psalmist tells himself three times. God loves us supremely, and he doesn't want us to hurt. Yet, he'll allow us to hurt if our pain draws us to his grace and to a deeper love relationship with him. Spiritual depression can become an occasion of discovering a deeper joy in God than we have ever known before.

There's often been a settled peace in my heart that sustained me when I fell into spiritual depression. I was able to hear from God, trusting that he would lead me, which indeed he did. Although God didn't speak to me audibly or through an angel, the word of God gave me encouragement. Even if angry with God, if we are still before him, a new God-awareness will lift us from our depression. We'll be reminded that he's our Savior, the Christ of the cross, who desires that we draw nearer to him, trusting in his loving purpose for us. His love and grace and delight in us will see to it that we abandon lesser enjoyments to find our true enjoyment in him. Our God loves us so much than in his holy zeal and jealousy he will not accept a secondary place in our hearts. He demands that we love him above all other loves and enjoy him above all other enjoyment.

The primary, most consistent emotion that we're to experience is joy, which is part of the fruit of the Spirit (Gal. 5:22f). We're commanded to rejoice in the Lord always (Phil. 4:4); and joy was a dominant emotion that characterized the disciples in the earliest church. They even rejoiced in the privilege of suffering disgrace and punishment for their faithful witness to Jesus (Acts 5:41). No doubt the joy of those earliest Christians was a big part of their appeal to the lost world around them.

Those with great earthly, temporal, material and physical (even good health) blessings, what we might term as good fortune, are not the most blessed people. Even those of us who belong to God's kingdom as his redeemed children might tend to think that these with happier circumstances are the blessed ones. But the psalmist discovered, and we too also will eventually realize that the most blessed people are those who have been driven into the arms of a loving God in desperate dependence, who find our greatest delight, joy and pleasure in him alone. If we only knew how much the Father loves us!

# Trusting God

## Psalm 139:1-18

> *O LORD, you have searched me and known me.*
> *² You know when I sit down and when I rise up;*
>   *you discern my thoughts from far away.*
> *³ You search out my path and my lying down,*
>   *and are acquainted with all my ways.*
> *⁴ Even before a word is on my tongue,*
>   *O LORD, you know it completely.*
> *⁵ You hem me in, behind and before,*
>   *and lay your hand upon me.*
> *⁶ Such knowledge is too wonderful for me;*
>   *it is so high that I cannot attain it.*
>
> *For it was you who formed my inward parts;*
>   *you knit me together in my mother's womb.*
> *¹⁴ I praise you, for I am fearfully and wonderfully made.*
>   *Wonderful are your works;*
> *that I know very well.*
> *¹⁵   My frame was not hidden from you,*
> *when I was being made in secret,*
>   *intricately woven in the depths of the earth.*
> *¹⁶ Your eyes beheld my unformed substance.*
> *In your book were written*
>   *all the days that were formed for me,*
>   *when none of them as yet existed.*
> *¹⁷ How weighty to me are your thoughts, O God!*
>   *How vast is the sum of them!*
> *¹⁸ I try to count them—they are more than the sand;*
>   *I come to the end—I am still with you.*

In this psalm, David's prays to God with an awareness of his perfect wisdom and powerful presence and concludes thereby that God is a God we can follow in a relationship of total trust.

Trust is sometimes hard to come by. In our daily life we have problems knowing whom to believe and whom to follow. Because of a history of broken promises, many have become cynical about politicians, who ask us to follow their leadership in government. People remember broken promises and failed leadership and thus are reluctant to follow those who seek to be leaders in government or in business.

Sadly, even in church life, because of the moral failure and hypocrisy of pastors, priests and other ministers, many are reluctant to follow their religious leaders, if indeed they have remained in their churches. Paul the apostle called for the people, some who had been prejudiced against his leadership, to follow him with a *conditional* follower-ship:

*"Follow my example, as I follow the example of Christ"* (1 Cor. 11:1).

We can follow leaders who themselves are accountable to a higher authority and example. After expressing his troubled thoughts as well as thoughts of praise for God's greatness, David gives a prayer of surrender to God, saying that, after his reflection in his prayer and meditation, he's now ready to surrender to God's leadership "in the way everlasting" (verse 24). But before he comes to that commitment, he struggles as he contemplates the attributes of God that lead him to this conclusion.

In the opening stanza of this psalm (1-6), David says that we can follow a God who knows all about us. He knows everything! David is first moved to think of God's omniscience, that he knows everything that happens in his creation, and God knows what has happened, what is happening and what is yet to take place.

God knows our thoughts and speech even before we think and open our mouths (2b & 4). David doesn't simply praise God for his omniscience; he also expresses his discomfort with the thought that he also judges us: "You hem me in," David says. David realizes that he is never out of God's sight, which is not always a comfortable thought. There are times when I wish God were not omniscient, when he didn't know my thoughts or my words. Frankly, at times I wish he would simply leave me alone and just be available when I need him and aware of me only when I'm on my best behavior. But the fact remains, God is always fully aware of all my thoughts, words and actions.

He, the perfectly righteous God is also the perfect judge. He sees beyond and behind all our actions, which we think will impress him and hide our hypocrisy from him, such as religious routine and observances. But Jesus, the eternal Son of God, sees beyond our rituals and when we are giving him just superficial lip service (Matt. 15:1ff; Is. 29:13). In his incarnation, the eternal Son laid aside his glory but not his full deity. Nathanael was amazed by Jesus' knowledge of what he was doing and where he was sitting even before Jesus met him (Jn. 1:47ff).

David says that this all-knowing God, even though he is the perfect Judge, has laid his hand upon him (5b). Peterson's *The Message* paraphrases this to say that God's hand upon David is indicative of his "reassuring presence, coming and going."

The good news is that, although God knows us completely and judges us perfectly, he also sympathizes compassionately with us. The Book of Hebrews reminds us that Jesus, the Son of God, is also our sympathetic great high priest (4:14-5:10). He who lived among us as one of us, knows all about our weaknesses and vulnerability. And as the great high priest he made the perfect sacrifice that satisfies the justice of a holy God who knows all about us. We can follow a God who knows all about us, loves us, gave his all for us, and who is always with us (7-12).

In the second stanza of the psalm, David says that *God is omnipresent:* He's everywhere, an amazing thought! The entire the creation, which defies all measurements, is filled with the presence of the creator/sustainer God. This is not pantheism. God is not the same as his creation but rather is beyond it and separate, though not in presence, from it. We know that God is spirit, as Jesus says (Jn. 4:24) and thus can be omnipresent, everywhere at the same time, except where he chooses to remove himself.

David seems to express a desire to flee from God, and there are times when we're uncomfortable at the thought of his presence. David was perhaps referring to the way he doubtless sought to flee into the darkness of secrecy, hiding from the presence of God after his egregious sin with Bathsheba and against her husband, Uriah (2 Sam. 11. Regardless of how we try to hide our sins or regardless of the spiritual darkness into which our souls may plunge, God is nevertheless present (11f).

You've perhaps heard the story of Francis Thompson (1859-1907), whose most famous poem, *The Hound of Heaven*, is an autobiographical description of how Christ pursued him like a hound until he graciously rescued him. When young Thompson failed in his efforts to become a priest, and then failed to become a medical doctor to please his parents; he then became a homeless drug addict, sleeping under a London bridge. In desperation he introduced himself and his literary work to a magazine editor and his wife, who recognized young Thompson's talent and took pity on this desperately sick and addicted young man. The Meynells admitted young Thompson into a monastery, where he could recover from his opium addiction and write poetry. There, in 1889, at the age of 30, Thompson wrote *The Hound of Heaven*, with some of the following lines:

> *I fled Him, down the nights and down the days;*
> *I fled Him, down the arches of the years;*
> *I fled Him, down the labyrinthine ways*
>   *Of my own mind; and in the mist of tears*
> *I hid from Him, and under running laughter.*

Francis Thompson was running from the loving God, who pursued him even against his will and then transformed his will and gave him hope. Our situation may not be as desperate as was young Thompson's, but nevertheless we may be emotionally and spiritually, if not physically running from God. But God is right here, and we cannot run away from him.

Soon after the Gulf War in Iraq, US Commanding General Norman Swartzkopf was interviewed on a late-night television program and described the behavior of his dog after it had badly misbehaved. The general said his dog, knowing he was guilty of disobedience and was facing discipline from his master, would cover his eyes with his paws. The dog thought that by blinding himself he was making himself disappear or become invisible to his master. And that's the same foolishness David describes in this psalm. We think that by plunging ourselves into spiritual darkness or going into some kind of "respectable hiding" here in Madison, we're making ourselves invisible to God, that he really won't notice our temporary disappearance. Just because we can no longer see God doesn't mean he can no longer see us. God will not countenance our self-ordered leave of absence from him. We are never on vacation from God and he's always seeking our love, worship and fellowship, and he expects, even demands, our loving faithfulness to him.

But wherever we try to go, God is there and, as David says he *will never leave us.* There seems to be a shift in mood, just as in the first stanza, from being uncomfortable with God's omniscience and omnipresence, to one of grateful surrender. At first David wants to hide and run from God. But then his attitude becomes one of gratitude for God's knowing, when he lays his hand of blessing on David (5b) and gratitude that God is present to guide him and hold him fast (10). As you read the story of David, you see that he was always in need of God's protection and deliverance from his enemies, whether the Philistines, King Saul, or even the enemies from his own household. He found great strength and encouragement in the awareness of God's presence.

For those who know and love God, this is a great comfort. God is always with us, alongside us and, through the Holy Spirit, dwelling in us. Regardless of how distant he may seem from us, we have the assurance that the risen Christ will never leave or forsake us and is with us always (Matt. 28:20). This is the will of the Triune God, that we might be with him forever (Jn. 17:24).

And David says that this God we can follow is still working on us (13-24). Beginning with the 13th verse, David turns his thoughts toward God's creation of him, and notes that God's greatness can be seen also in his creation of a human being, the crown of all his creation.

Scientist/evangelist Louie Giglio presents a powerful portrayal of the wonderful complexity of the human body, with its some 75 trillion cells and that replace themselves with remarkable rapidity. He also remarks that the human eye is "the most technically advanced piece of equipment on the planet." Giglio speaks about the remarkable laminin protein in the human body that literally holds the human body together and shows how this protein is in the shape of a cross. This may well be God's imprint to remind us of what Paul says, that Christ is the image of the invisible God, by whom all things were created and in him all things hold together (Col. 1:15ff). Christ is the great creator of a vast, unknowable universe and of intricate, fearfully made human beings. And he didn't just create us—he also holds us together and cares deeply about each one of us

David acknowledges that his body was created by God and the days of his life were foreknown by this Creator, who shaped him into his own image, as God's *eikons* (Gr. "images").

Several years ago, on a visit to Florence, I stood in awe before the great masterpiece of Michelangelo, his most famous sculpture, *David*. Our artist and art professor daughter, Stephanie, helped me to appreciate the brilliance of this masterpiece with her comments about its amazing proportions and attention to detail. I was particularly interested in learning that Michelangelo created this masterpiece from a huge block of marble that had been abandoned in the late fifteenth century by the Florentine sculptor, Agostino d'Antonio, who gave up on working with this piece of marble as being hopeless because of a fatal flaw in the marble. When the young Michelangelo found this block of marble, it was not only flawed but by now badly disfigured from d'Antonio's truncated efforts. But Michelangelo "saw beyond the ugly disfigured block of marble to the magnificent sculpture he knew he could create. As a result, he began his work. The final statue—the celebrated *David*—is widely regarded as one of the most outstanding artistic achievements of all time" (Joanna and Alister McGrath).

With all his flaws and sins, David experienced the redeeming, image-restoring work of God's Spirit. His prayer for God to search, know and test him, reveal his sinful, harmful ways to him and then lead him in the way everlasting is a prayer for this work of redemption (23f). God sees us in the same way—not as we are in our sin, rebellion, iniquity and failure—but as we will become by his grace and Spirit. He looks beyond all our flaws and the cracks in the *eikon*, the image of God, and sees us as righteous as Christ is righteous. He also begins at work on us immediately to begin shaping us into his masterpieces, his image bearers, far more precious in his sight than any human-made masterpiece.

In the closing verses of this great psalm, David has come to a point of fresh surrender to following the Lord God in "the way everlasting," the way of eternal life that's a pilgrimage to the everlasting new heaven and earth, the city of God. We can trust that God will lead us to the fulfillment of this great and solid hope, which is not wishful thinking but strong, well-founded conviction. Our God is a God we can follow and trust all the way into eternity.

# The Money Choice

## Matthew 6:19-24

> *19 "Do not store up for yourselves treasures on earth, where moth and rust consume and where thieves break in and steal; 20 but store up for yourselves treasures in heaven, where neither moth nor rust consumes and where thieves do not break in and steal. 21 For where your treasure is, there your heart will be also.*
>
> *22 "The eye is the lamp of the body. So, if your eye is healthy, your whole body will be full of light; 23 but if your eye is unhealthy, your whole body will be full of darkness. If then the light in you is darkness, how great is the darkness!*
>
> *24 "No one can serve two masters; for a slave will either hate the one and love the other or be devoted to the one and despise the other. You cannot serve God and wealth.*

One of my favorite cartoons shows two men walking out of church, looking shell-shocked, and wearing nothing but a barrel to conceal their nakedness. One said to the other, "That was the best stewardship sermon I've ever heard!"

You don't need to hold onto your clothes or even your wallets for this sermon. Possibly because some preachers use the bully pulpit to say too much about giving shouldn't overrule the fact that Jesus spoke about money more frequently than any other subject except the kingdom of God. Jesus understood the relationship between the spiritual and the material, the attitude we have toward kingdom of God values and the attitude we have toward the values of this fallen world in which we live. Jesus is Lord of our finances as well as Lord of our worship, prayer life and relationships with others. As the great Reformer, Martin Luther said, "There are three conversions necessary: the conversion of the heart, mind and the purse."

I tend to agree with the scholar who said that perhaps the greatest danger to Western Christianity is not forces and ideologies alien to our faith, such as Islam, the New Age Movement or atheistic humanism, but "the all-pervasive materialism of our affluent culture" (Blomberg). We encounter this mindset of self-serving consumerism, which erodes generosity and sacrificial giving and discourages the willingness to follow Jesus at all costs. Even we Christians continue to overspend on ourselves, sometimes oblivious to the many in the world are in abject poverty and dying of starvation.

Jesus' teachings about making the right money choice was not a sermon to the wealthy, but to folks who probably were a lot poorer than just about all of us here today. The First Century knew very few rich Christians. The dangers of riches and materialism face not only the rich but also those who want to get rich (1Tim. 6:9). We all need to beware of the insidious influence of materialism, even in the Christian culture. We have the same temptation as the First Century Jews of thinking that our material prosperity is a sure and certain sign that we are on good terms with God. And so, we erroneously equate our spiritual condition with our financial position.

Jesus gives us the negative command to not store up treasures on earth, where moth and rust consume, and where thieves break in and steal" (19). Jesus may well have been referring to clothing and tapestries, which were valuable commodities used in trading, commerce and as investments for the future, much like tapestries were used in Medieval Europe and valuable antiques are used today. These items were subject to natural deterioration, and money, which usually was hidden away in homes, was subject to thievery from robbers who could dig through earthen walls.

We who are followers of Jesus are also people of the earth and are compelled and responsible to make some earthly provisions for ourselves and those who depend on us, namely our families. Scripture tells us that we are to be industrious and save up for the future (Prov. 6:6ff) and that we're to provide for our families' financial and material needs. To not do so, Paul says, is to be "worse than an unbeliever" (1 Tim. 5:8).

But as followers of Jesus we're to be aware of the folly of placing all our hopes and all our stock in the earthly, which is subject to erosion (declining investments) and theft (loss of savings). As we pray in the Lord's Prayer, we're dependent on the heavenly Father for our daily bread, daily provisions of the material. We've learned from financial crises that no investments are safe from erosion and theft. And nothing we own of the material is ours or even our heirs, forever. As was said following the death of a billionaire, "How much did he leave?" Answer: "He left it all." In Jesus' Parable of the Rich Fool, God called the man a fool who accumulated real estate wealth to the neglect of his soul (Lk. 12:20).

Having given the negative command, Jesus gives the positive. The Jews of Jesus' audience were familiar with the language of making Kingdom of God investments. Doing God's commands was understood by many of the faithful to be the equivalent to accumulating treasures with God, and in this context, obeying God's commands included acts of charity. Jesus says that the right, the only safe investment is what we give to heavenly, eternal causes. There is a way we can make a certain investment that will not be subject to erosion or loss. When we use the material to invest in people, we gain eternal favor. Jesus says that our hearts—love, interest, attention and affection—follow our investments, our treasure (21). Inordinate attention to money and material matters draws our hearts into the grips of materialism and idolatry. But investing in people puts our hearts in the right place.

When we make financial investments, we need good insight into the position and reliability of the company or institution through which we invest. Jesus speaks about the need to a good eye for investments in the truly worthwhile and the eternal. Jesus speaks of the necessity of being able to see things clearly, from a kingdom of God perspective. This is infinitely more important than having the best of financial advisors.

Note how Jesus assessed the widow's offering (Lk. 21:1-4). The gifts of the rich didn't impress Jesus at all. He knew they were giving out of great wealth, what they had left over and how little sacrifice they were making. But also, Jesus commended the superior giving of the poor widow, whose offering of "two very small copper coins" represented all she had to live on. Jesus allowed and blessed this sacrificial faith gift and knew that the heavenly Father would provide for this poor widow and bless her abundantly. Jesus' eyes could see real sacrifice, faith and the assurance of the Father's provisions. Good eyes can see to be generous, sacrificial and trusting. "Outlook determines outcome" (Wiersbe).

Good eyes can also see that there's nothing inherently evil in the financial and the material. Many misquote Scripture to say that money is the root of all evil, when in fact Paul says that the love of money is the root of all kinds of evil (1 Tim. 6:10). And in the same section Paul, dismissing the idea that disciples are ascetics, says that God "richly provides us with everything for our enjoyment (17). Paul says that if we are blessed with riches (and he would think of just about all of us here today as rich), we're not to arrogantly put our hope in them but rather in God. We're to be rich in good deeds, generous and willing to share. We're to hold onto riches loosely and be ready and willing to use them, keep them and give them away. In this way, he says, we're laying up treasures in heaven (18f).

To the Corinthian church Paul encouraged their generosity based on the grace of the Lord Jesus, who is our supreme example in giving (2 Cor. 8:9). He also reminded them of the law of the harvest that says that we cannot out-give God. God's grace stays ahead of us and provides for us, enabling us to continue to live and give generously (2 Cor. 9:6-15).

One of the crassest expressions of the bad, blind eyes of materialism is seen on some bumper stickers: "He who dies with the most toys wins." Wins what? Obviously, this philosophy makes life a game of the acquisition of things. Jesus would say life is no game, and that the materialist who treats it as such loses his own soul for eternity (Lk. 12:20). We use the world's thinking in the way we speak of the value of someone. When we hear of the death of a rich and famous person, we ask, "How much was he worth?" We ascribed worth to a human being based on her or his financial status.

Those without the mind and eyes of Christ simply cannot see the "benefits" of investing in kingdom of God causes. The idea of "God's miraculous plan of economy" is absurd to them, including the law of the harvest and that says one cannot out-give God. A bad eye is unable to see the value and experience the joy of giving. A bad eye overvalues the temporal and the material and forgets the value of the eternal and the spiritual, as did the rich fool in Jesus' parable (Lk. 12:13-21). The bad eye neglects the needy, like the rich man who neglected Lazarus at the peril and loss of his own soul (Lk. 16:19-31).

I've never been good at deciding money matters; and so, for that purpose long ago I decided I need a professional money manager to give advice, especially as we planned for our children's support through university and toward their own financial independence. The right money choice involves the right investments, assessments and now, management. Will we let God and his word manage our resources or will we let money itself manage us? Jesus says in the final verse of our text that we face the choice of serving God or being enslaved by money. Jesus says we cannot have it both ways. We either serve God or we serve Money, with a capital "M."

"Wealth" is a translation of the Aramaic term "Mammon," which has a personal character, personifying a rival god and not just some impersonal medium of currency. Jesus says we either serve God our heavenly Father or we serve the god called Mammon or Money. If we are not committed to the Lordship of Christ we'll be under the dominion of Mammon, a god who will control us and divert us from God's kingdom. We can't have it both ways. For this reason, Jesus commanded the Rich Young Man to sell his possession, give to the poor and then follow him. Jesus commanded him to break free from the god of Mammon, who held him in his grip. Apart from the grace of God it's impossible, Jesus says, for the rich who serve Mammon to enter the kingdom. It would be "easier for a camel to go through the eye of a needle than for a rich man to enter the kingdom of God" (Matt. 19:24).

Someone has said that money is a great servant but a horrible master. If we're not serving God with our money we're under the dominion of Mammon. If we give God the leftovers after we've indulged our own interests and served our personal priorities, we're living in disobedience and practicing idolatry. Everything we have he has entrusted to us. We're to enjoy life and our possessions but keep them subservient to the Lordship of Christ and realize he's the owner of all things. Our houses, cars, salaries and all our possessions are his. We must hold onto things loosely and use them in his service and be prepared to leave them or give them away.

A man and his son were walking to church one Sunday and the father gave his son two quarters (in a time when a quarter could buy a candy bar), one of which was to go into the offering plate at church and the other could be used for candy on the way home after church. As they walked over a sewer grate on the sidewalk, the boy lost his grip on the coins and one of them fell through the iron grate into oblivion. "Oops," he exclaimed. "There goes God's quarter!"

When we fail to give God the first-fruits, off the top of our earnings, we usually give the leftovers. The practice of tithing was a recognition of God's ownership through giving him "off the top" of our earnings. Unless we're committed to faithful stewardship and kingdom priorities, in a time of financial "pinch" we're likely to say, "Oops, there goes God's money, what I would have given to his cause." Kingdom giving is faith giving, not asking what we can afford, but first asking what we can trust God to enable us to give.

I suppose the question we must ask ourselves, when we think about this money choice is, "Who owns us?" Who owns you, God or your money? If God doesn't own, you then you cannot really own your money. It owns you, regardless how much is on your accounts or your pocket. A billionaire was asked, "How much money does it take to make you happy?" "A little bit more," he said quite honestly. We need to realize that Jesus alone gives us the abundant life (John 10:10). Only Jesus can deliver us from the snares of the material, even those of us of more modest means who erroneously think we're immune from these snares.

Our guarantee of provision is the love of God shown us in Jesus and the cross. Paul called the Corinthians to remember "the grace of our Lord Jesus Christ, that though he was rich, yet for (our) sakes he became poor, so that (we) through his poverty might become rich" (2 Cor. 8:9). Because of his love for us, we today enjoy the abundance of kingdom of God living and the assurance of his ongoing provision (Matt. 6:33; Rom. 8:32). We have this choice, to give ourselves first and then our money and all our possessions to him (2 Cor. 8:5) who loved us and gave himself for us. Let's make the right money choice.

# Jesus' Invitation to Rest

## Matthew 11:25-30

> $^{25}$ At that time Jesus said, "I thank you, Father, Lord of heaven and earth, because you have hidden these things from the wise and the intelligent and have revealed them to infants; $^{26}$ yes, Father, for such was your gracious will. $^{27}$ All things have been handed over to me by my Father; and no one knows the Son except the Father, and no one knows the Father except the Son and anyone to whom the Son chooses to reveal him.
>
> $^{28}$ "Come to me, all you that are weary and are carrying heavy burdens, and I will give you rest. $^{29}$ Take my yoke upon you and learn from me; for I am gentle and humble in heart, and you will find rest for your souls. $^{30}$ For my yoke is easy, and my burden is light."

A friend of ours, who with her husband has served in ministry to the point of exhaustion, in desperation finally visited a professional counselor. His immediate diagnosis was that she had worked herself to total exhaustion. The counselor said that unless she changed her ways of constant work and stress she would be dead in two months' time. If not to this dangerous extent, there likely are some here, possibly even retirees, who need rest, and not just by sleeping in on Sunday mornings, as is the manner of some.

In my youth and early ministry, church busyness seemed to be of great value in spiritual formation. In my pastor-father's home, we attended a plethora of weekly and sometimes daily church meetings and activities. I even recall a conference preacher bragging about how he kept the people in his church busy attending meetings and performing tasks, even to the point of exhaustion. He disclosed his theory that "Busy Baptists don't sin as much." I wasn't so sure then, and I'm certainly not in accord with this statement now. Church busyness can indeed become a preoccupation that keeps Baptists and others away from taverns and other places often designated as sinful, but busy Baptists can devise other ways to be sinful, even in church. During church busyness, we can be ungodly and judgmental toward others. During seminary days, I served my first church on busy weekends, ending with a Sunday evening service before driving back to Louisville for another week of studies. Preaching on humility, I misquoted Jesus' promise that those who humble themselves in service "will be exalted." I said, almost unconsciously, "shall be exhausted"!

The Old Covenant Sabbath laws were provided to give God's people rest. But the Sabbath was a prefiguring of a greater rest that is to be found in a relationship with God, something that many Israelites forfeited (Ps. 95:11).

Jesus invites us to enter God's rest through faith in him (Heb. 4:1-11). Jesus praised the Father for revealing his invitation to the willing, those he described as "little children," those who realized their need for him. These are the "ordinary people" (Peterson), those Paul describes as the most likely candidates for God's salvation rest. The willing are those who're aware of their need and who are weary of an empty, futile life.

The weary that Jesus addressed included those weighed down by religious demands, some 613 laws that the Jewish teachers had mined from the Old Covenant Scriptures and their oral tradition (28). The faith of Israel had become a great burden because the joy and the music had been drowning out by legalistic requirements. The call of God to a personal relationship had been drowned out by the harsh demands of law and traditions that were impossibly demanding.

In the church of today there are many so-called Christians who are weary and tired of trying to live by their or others' expectations, and they simply can't measure up. They're described by Paul's weary condition, when he tried by his efforts to keep the law and failed to do what he should have and couldn't stop doing what he shouldn't have. "What a wretched man I am! Who will rescue me from this body of death?" (Rom. 7:24). Such weary people, and I confess I too easily slip into their company, are simply missing out on the joy of Jesus' rest because a love relationship with Christ has been replaced by performance demands, beginning in childhood with our parents. There are lots of church people doing lots of church work without joy and purpose.

*The Message* paraphrases a part of our text with these words: "Are you tired? Worn out? Burned out on religion?" and indeed I have seen a lot of people who were burned out, not because of what Jesus was doing *through* them, but by what they were trying, frenetically and legalistically, to do *for* him. They've lost the music singing, dancing and joy Christ came to give because of the rules and expectations we placed on ourselves and others. Christ has come to set us free from the condemnation and burden of the law and has set us free with the joy of his forgiveness and the presence and power of his life and Spirit to enable us to live a full and meaningful life (Jn. 10:10) in the joy and freedom of the Spirit (Rom. 8:1ff).

In our culture, instead of the burden of legalism, many are heavy laden with immorality and the real guilt that accompanies a life with no moral absolutes or restraint. Chuck Colson was conversing with a young lady, who had obviously become weary of a life of self-indulgence and non-stop partying. She had come to believe that she was obligated to live a hedonistic life-style of unrestrained pleasure, which obviously was losing its pleasure for her. When Chuck explained to her about God's forgiveness and that she could follow Christ in a life of loving obedience to his plan and will, she asked in amazement, "Do you mean I don't have to do what I want to do?" She spoke for the many who are burdened down with the bondage and emptiness of the meaningless pursuit of sensual pleasure and addictions. Jesus can set us free from the bondage of such a so-called hedonistic "freedom."

The willing are the burdened (28) from sin and guilt, and realize their need for forgiveness, whether from overt sins of the flesh or the sin of proud religious performance. Some are tired of trying to live up to the expectations of others and of trying to prove their worth to themselves or to others.

Those who are invited are the weary—religious and secular, church people and those outside the realm of religious faith. And as a long-time believer, follower and servant of Christ, I'm all too aware of my weariness from ignoring the rest Jesus offers. As G Campbell Morgan says, all restlessness is godlessness, and most of us carry burdens we're not supposed to carry, such as the burdens of bitterness and anger towards others or even towards God for life's disappointments and pain.

Jesus promises his rest to all who come to him. This is the language of faith and trust and of a personal relationship with Christ that results in his salvation rest. Scripture speaks a lot about the rest of salvation that we receive in Christ, which is the rest of sins forgiven and a life of trust in Christ and a hope of perfect everlasting rest with Christ for all eternity (Hebrews). He invites us to the rest of freedom from anxiety and fear as we learn to trust him, who replaces our restlessness with his peace-instilling presence. We learn to cast all our anxieties upon him, knowing that he cares for us (1 Pet. 5:7). In our relationship with Christ, we receive the peace that transcends all understanding (Phil. 4:7). Our rest from guilt, anxiety, restlessness, fear, bitterness and a sense of worthlessness doesn't come through human effort or psychotherapy, but rather through a relationship of faith and trust in Jesus.

FW Robertson noted that there are three causes of unrest: 1) suspicion of God, 2) inward discord and 3) dissatisfaction with outward circumstances. Jesus invites us to bring all of these to him. Maybe there is a suspicion of God, and a doubt of his steadfast love and faithfulness toward you. Perhaps its' time we revisit the cross, to be reminded of the unfailing and absolute love of God. Maybe there's inward discord, a spiritual or moral struggle within our hearts. We can't have God's peace until we relinquish all compromise with sin and self-will. Perhaps there's a dissatisfaction with our outward circumstances that causes inward rebellion or resentment. If so, we need to ask God for grace to trust that we are exactly where we ought to be and our circumstances have come to us through the permission of a loving God.

Ironically, in his invitation to rest Jesus invites us to take his yoke upon us. This is figurative language. Scholars say that as a carpenter's son, Jesus doubtless made wooden yokes that were tailor made to the shape of the oxen, to insure greatest ease and comfort to the animals as they pulled the burden of the ox cart.

There might even have been a sign over Joseph's carpenter's shop which read, "My yoke fits well" (Barclay).

Jesus invites us to join him in his service, but first, to a well-fitting personal relationship with him whereby we are yoked to him in a life of glad service. He invites us first to know and learn from him, who is "gentle and humble in heart" (29). As CH Spurgeon points out, this is the only place in Scripture that refers to the heart of Jesus, and how precious this is for us. And only Jesus, the divine and eternal Son of God, could refer to himself as humble. He, the Lord of glory, humbled himself in his incarnation and all the way to death on the cross (Phil. 2:6-8). Jesus invites us to know his heart in the most intimate of personal relationships, which, alas, is one we often neglect. Jesus invites us to learn true humility from him as we yoke up with him in living in the Father's will and doing the Father's work.

Thus, the rest to which Jesus invites us is not inaction or passivity. He calls us to a life that is humanly impossible and one that can be lived only by dependence on his grace and the Holy Spirit. We can't, and we shouldn't try to live this life in our strength, but only as we are properly yoked up with Christ Jesus and learning of him and becoming more like him day by day. This easy yoke and light burden is what reminds me of something I heard that The Great Awakening Leader and founder of Methodism, John Wesley (1703-91), is reported to have said: "I grow weary *in* my work but never weary *of* it."

Even when we grow weary in mind and body, in step with Jesus, our strength is renewed (Is. 40:31). The rest we have in Jesus is through a relationship with him when we're aware of him and living by his grace and power at work in us. This is how we can be at rest and peace even as we labor with him. His yoke will fit us well. We're not to become weary in doing good, as Paul writes (Gal. 6:9). The answer is not to retreat into resignation and indifference or allow ourselves to become totally burned out to and embittered toward the work of God and his people. The answer is to return to Jesus and to submit to his well-fitting yoke.

Jesus may be inviting you to take a time of spiritual retreat, to take an inventory of your life and activities that seem to deprive you of your spiritual rest. You'll find rest through personal and corporate worship, which keep Jesus central in your thoughts. To get things sorted out, take a personal retreat, perhaps for an overnight, or at least a morning or day in prayer and reflection.

Jesus invites us all to his rest and to join him under his restful yet useful and fruitful yoke of service. What we're talking about is being aware of Jesus' presence and being led by the Holy Spirit. The Savior lovingly invites us to repent of our weariness from doing good *for* him instead of restfully and graciously doing work *with* him. He invites all of us who are weary and burdened. Let's find our rest in him.

I'm glad our faithful religious worker friend is finding rest in Jesus, physically, emotionally and spiritually. I'm glad she has a good, wise and godly counselor. Perhaps you need one too. In any and every case, we all need to accept Jesus' invitation to his rest.

# Jesus' Call to Follow Him

## Mark 1:14-20

> *¹⁴ Now after John was arrested, Jesus came to Galilee, proclaiming the good news of God, ¹⁵ and saying, "The time is fulfilled, and the kingdom of God has come near; repent, and believe in the good news."*
>
> *¹⁶ As Jesus passed along the Sea of Galilee, he saw Simon and his brother Andrew casting a net into the sea—for they were fishermen. ¹⁷ And Jesus said to them, "Follow me and I will make you fish for people."¹⁸ And immediately they left their nets and followed him. ¹⁹ As he went a little farther, he saw James son of Zebedee and his brother John, who were in their boat mending the nets. ²⁰ Immediately he called them; and they left their father Zebedee in the boat with the hired men and followed him.*

Often through the church's preaching, teaching and religious vocabulary, we layer over the clear words of Jesus with our own interpretations and traditions. When we hear "call" or "calling to discipleship" we're likely to associate these words with a vocational calling to ministry in the church or through missionary service. And indeed, there are special callings in the gospels and in the kingdom of God today. In our text, Jesus was calling the inner circle of his disciples, three of whom would become leaders in the earliest church after Jesus ascension back into heaven. But as Mark relates this call of Jesus, he intends for all his readers to consider that God calls each of is to a lifetime of following, learning and apprenticeship in Kingdom living and serving.

Jesus called his first disciples and he calls us because he desires an everlasting love relationship with us. This is a wonder of his grace, that Jesus should want our love and fellowship, not only now but for all eternity (John 17:20-26). We need to realize the inestimable privilege, that Jesus invites us to follow and be with him forever. And Jesus' purpose was to call others to tell his saving message and be agents of his saving work even after his death, resurrection and ascension back into heaven.

Jesus spoke to these disciples with his ultimate authority as Lord of all. This was one of the striking aspects of Jesus' ministry. Although he came to us in all humility, lowliness and the unpretentiousness of a Galilean peasant, when Jesus spoke, his message resounded with authority. Those he addressed recognized something of God's authority in his voice and in his teaching, which was lacking in the ostentatious pronouncements of the religious authorities (Mark 1:22; Matthew 7:29).

Jesus spoke with the authority of God because he was God incarnate, a claim that critical unbelievers could not accept or even tolerate. And with that divine authority, Jesus took the initiative in calling his disciples to abandon other competing commitments to follow him in absolute surrender and unqualified obedience. Jesus spoke like a commanding officer, and those who believed in him realized that to demur or even hesitate would be an act of high treason. Do we also hear the voice of the one who created all and is Lord overall and whose reign someday shall be acknowledged by all?

The criteria he used in calling these first disciples seemed almost indiscriminate. He didn't look for followers who had a theological education or even much formal training of any kind. Although the first disciples certainly were not ignoramuses or underachievers, they nevertheless were regarded by the religious elite as "ordinary men with no special training" (Acts 4:13).

In 1988, I was part of a group of four pastors from our city who were invited by a local TV station to travel to Israel to film a special on the life of Jesus. We were all given four or five speaking segments to be filmed in fitting locations. One of mine, since I was the Baptist in the group, was to speak about the baptism of Jesus as we stood on the mouth of the Jordan near Lake Galilee. As soon as we finished that film shoot, a boat-full of young fisherman arrived in their large wooden boat, not much different from those of Jesus' day, except for a small trolling motor. These young men were excited about an obviously successful catch of fish, as they tossed their catch into the back of a pick-up truck and drove away. As I saw their youthful vigor, heard their laughter, likely sprinkled with a few choice words, I thought, "These guys are like the young men

Jesus called." Jesus sought after the ordinary so that, in the words of the Apostle Paul, he would thereby show the world that the extraordinary power of the kingdom is from God and not from human ability (1 Cor. 1:18-2:5).

Jesus had already introduced himself to these disciples, and it's possible that they'd been with him for as long as a year, watching him minister and hearing him teach (Jn. 1:35-51). Yet now was the time for them to draw nearer in a closer love-relationship of total commitment to him. To follow Jesus would demand they now accept responsibility in sharing his mission and prepare to continue his work.

I pray that I'm resolved to know Jesus in a closer love and trust relationship, hopefully drawing nearer to the aspiration of the apostle Paul, who said that his desire was to know Christ in a deeper, more satisfying and life-changing relationship. But the longer I live and observe the lives of those who yearn to know Christ in a deeper way, I realize what a costly objective this is. Paul linked his expression of desire in knowing Christ and the power of his resurrection with the necessity of "the fellowship of sharing in his sufferings" and "becoming like him in his death" (Phil. 3:10).

To follow Jesus, to walk in his steps, means to take up our cross daily, which is the cruciform life of saying "no" to self-centered, self-directed lives and a willingness to share in Jesus' reproach, rejection and suffering (Luke 9:23 & 1 Peter 2.21). The more we live conscious of his presence the more of his character becomes our character, his virtues our virtues. As we abide in him as a branch abides in the vine, the more fruit of the Spirit flows from our lives (John 15:1ff; Galatians 5:22f). And, to draw us closer to his loving presence, our heavenly Father may give Satan a longer tether (Job 1:6ff) to test, refine and strengthen us in him (Hebrews 12:4ff). He may allow some of our cherished and even godly dreams to be shattered to draw us yet closer to his love (Crabb).

To follow Jesus means not only that we live in communion with him but also that we are in close fellowship with his people. As these disciples, later to be joined by eight others, were called together as well as to follow Jesus, so are we called into a local fellowship, the church of Jesus, the Body of Christ on earth. We cannot be his followers without being drawn to and even mutually dependent on each other.

Fishing was a joint venture, a team effort, and Jesus told these disciples that he would send them out to fish for people just as they'd been fishing for fish for their livelihood (19). To fish for others was a metaphor that spoke clearly to these fishermen and not so vividly for us. These men knew all about the work of fishing, and that it required hard work, persistence, courage, patience, skill, teamwork, alertness and faith, since they couldn't see the fish! Joining Jesus in his kingdom work as his missional people, of bringing others to faith that they become his worshipers, requires our absolute dependence on his divine power. And it requires that we join with God's people in this endeavor.

Fishing in Lake Galilee was and still is a team effort, throwing overboard a heavy net, weighted at the four corners with heavy weights, that allow the nets to descend over a large catch of fish that requires a mighty effort to bring again to the surface. So, don't think of fishing for men as being analogous to your sitting under a shade tree on a lazy riverbank, dangling your worm on a hook from your cane pole. We need each other and especially we need God's grace, strength, wisdom and protection.

And so, for us as well, to be involved in kingdom work is to acknowledge that we can do nothing without the grace, power, wisdom and love of the Lord Jesus (John 15:5). And one thing that I have learned if nothing else—I am helpless and useless in the kingdom of God apart from the power of the Holy Spirit. And I know that the "sea" where we are called to fish, namely Madison and wherever God places us, requires his power, wisdom and anointing for a successful catch of "fish."

As one well-known African American preacher says in his colorfully way, Jesus has called us to be fishers of people, but we have instead settled for being keepers of an aquarium (EV Hill).

Jesus used this analogy of fishing for people because these first disciples were fishermen. But he would use different words for our following him. It's doing whatever will draw people to Jesus, involving the entire work and expression of the good news of Jesus, which includes his work of loving, caring, giving, and simple acts of kindness and mercy.

Jesus called these disciples to forsake their preoccupations and any other obstacles to following him unreservedly. For them it meant leaving behind the family business, which we can assume was successful. It also meant forsaking their partnership with their father and, we can assume, other family and community relationships. Probably for most of us following Jesus will not necessitate our changing occupations or even our address. But it will mean changing our preoccupation with self-centered objectives and making others the top priority of our lives.

We need to pause and think about the benefits of following Jesus. Just for starters we can say that the life of following Jesus is one of knowing and enjoying a soul-satisfying relationship with him. These four disciples, perhaps during their year of being with Jesus, had realized the joy of his presence and were willing to relinquish the lesser joys of a self-directed life without him. We shouldn't think of the life of following Jesus as the throwing away of life but rather as the discovery of a purposeful life that only God can give us (John 10:10; Matthew 10:39)

How do we know if we're following Jesus? Only if we can say that Jesus is Lord over our relationships, our jobs, our finances, our family life, and our free time can we have assurance we're following him. The obedience of these disciples stands in marked contrast with the fickle crowd, who came only to be "blessed" by Jesus, as he mercifully fed them and preformed miracles before them. When Jesus began to talk with them about a costly life of commitment to a life-changing relationship, "many of his disciples turned back and no longer followed him." But Peter and the others who continued to follow him understood that a life of following Jesus was the only option for eternal life (John 6:66-69).

When Jesus called these fishermen to follow, they obeyed. The time comes when action is required. Even to delay is to disobey. The call of God will never come at a time of personal convenience to us, but will always seem to be a rude, even unwelcome interruption.

Look at the biblical examples, of Gideon, who was called while busily threshing wheat (Judges 6:11ff); Elisha was occupied with plowing (1 Kings 19:19); Amos was taking care of his sheep and sycamore-fig trees (Amos 7:14) and Matthew was tending his tax collecting business (Matthew 9:9). They also received "no polite, reasoned invitation" but instead were issued an "unconditional, unexplained demand" (Turner).

Although we must count the cost, we can't know all the details or answer all the questions about what following Jesus will demand. And we know we'll never "feel ready," or that the time is right. There are too many details, attachments and complexities in our lives to wait for the "right time." The cost we are to count is the quality of our faith and strength of our commitment to follow Jesus. Will that last through the fiery battles and times of intense disappointment and loneliness? But to have all the details answered, everyone else satisfied with our decision—these are things that cannot wait but must rather be severed from our hearts as distractions and obstacles to ready obedience.

Jesus' calling had no time limit. When Jesus calls us to follow he doesn't negotiate for our retirement date and pension account. For these four, following Jesus involved a lifetime of obedience, service, suffering, exile and martyrdom. They followed Jesus to the end and since the end of their mortal pilgrimage have been enjoying the presence of Jesus and the fullness of the joy of paradise. How sadly mistaken are those who say they've put in their allotment of time in serving the Lord and now it's time for someone else to take over their service or ministry! Since when does anyone of us ever follow or serve Jesus enough?

I read with interest an interview of Judi Dench, successful and highly acclaimed actress. Some of you sophisticates might recognize her as a Shakespearean actress, and others of us as James Bond's boss. Dame Dench, well into in her 70's, and suffering from macular degeneration, is nevertheless in great demand for theatre and cinema roles. Asked by the interviewer if she was considering retiring, she replied, "No, no, no! I wouldn't. If you're in the minority of people who really want to do the work they're doing and you're lucky enough to be given a chance to do it then why stop? The whole discipline of learning is terribly good for us," she continued. "...I'm learning every single day." Citing her opportunities to work under new directors, she said, It's a learning curve all the time. I think that's very, very good for you and very important; it's like everlasting school in a way."

You and I are privileged to follow Jesus and learn from him and use our gifts with him in the everlasting school of the Kingdom. We too should say "No, no, no!" to the thought of retiring from the school of following Jesus. What does it mean for you to follow him, today?

# When Storms Come

## Mark 4:35-41

*On that day, when evening had come, he said to them, "Let us go across to the other side." *[36]* And leaving the crowd behind, they took him with them in the boat, just as he was. Other boats were with him.*[37]* A great windstorm arose, and the waves beat into the boat, so that the boat was already being swamped.*[38]* But he was in the stern, asleep on the cushion; and they woke him up and said to him, "Teacher, do you not care that we are perishing?" *[39]* He woke up and rebuked the wind, and said to the sea, "Peace! Be still!" Then the wind ceased, and there was a dead calm.* [40]* He said to them, "Why are you afraid? Have you still no faith?" *[41]* And they were filled with great awe and said to one another, "Who then is this, that even the wind and the sea obey him?"*

I wonder how I would have reacted to the storm had I been with Jesus and his disciples. Would I have responded with fear or with faith? I think you'll agree that we're living in a stormy time. Besides the storms of warfare and international terrorism and threats such as from North Korea, perhaps there are other storms raging or at least brewing in our lives. Our text forces us to ask, "How are we reacting?" Storms will come our way and into our lives. Will we react with faith or with fear?

Throughout Scripture the sea represents the perilous and that which is out of control. Life's storms will always threaten us. John and the other disciples could tell you that if you spend any time at all on Galilee you'll be in a storm. James, writing in his letter, didn't say, "If you face trials of many kinds," but rather he said, "whenever you face trials of many kinds" (James 1:2). Maybe your storms have to do with your or a loved-one's health. Maybe it's emotional, financial or relational. Sometimes the storm of life is when nothing at all seems to be happening for us, and we begin to think that life's opportunities are passing us by. You know your storms and maybe you alone know them. Maybe you can't discuss them with anyone.

Life's storms come suddenly and without warning. In Matthew's account of our text (Matthew 8:24) we read, "Without warning a furious storm came up." Imagine the fear in the hearts of these disciples! They viewed the waters as not only threatening but as an evil force, under the control of the enemy. They feared storms and the sea because they represented the demonic, the unknown, the uncontrollable, and the unwelcome. The storms in your life will seem senseless also. Yet God can bring good out of evil. God can put sense into the storm. In our text Jesus knew a storm was coming. And, he directed the disciples to get into the boat, knowing it was headed into a storm. Yet, from the disciples' perspective, the storm meant the loss of not only their new venture with Jesus, but also the loss of their lives.

Right now, the storm you are experiencing or facing probably makes no sense to you. You've worked hard to get where you are and now you have a pink slip that says you lost your job. You and your spouse always enjoyed good health, but now the doctor says otherwise. Maybe your storm isn't so much what's happened to you, but what hasn't happened, that is, your unfulfilled hopes. And often the timing of the storms seems senseless, when we're either already at the capacity of our endurance, along comes another storm.

And, as was the case with Jonah, the storms of our lives can be the result, the consequence of our disobedience. And because our God is a sovereign God of love and grace, he can and will deliver us from our self-induced problems, difficulties and storms. God loves his children, and if we won't return to him in the calm of life, he'll allow the storm as a wake-up call.

The disciples were in a storm because of their obedience. Jesus called them to join him in the boat headed for the storm. In his sovereign permission, God allows the storms that he can use in a redemptive, purposeful way, as part of his loving discipline in our lives. He uses storms to teach us to trust his love and care (2 Corinthians 12:9). The disciples' first response to the storm was fear. I'm not so sure my response would have been any different.

Fear is an initial response and an emotion. But faith is a decision. In the 53rd Psalm David said, "When I am afraid, I put my trust in you. In God, whose word I praise, in God I trust; I am not afraid; what can flesh do to me?" Notice, David didn't say, "If I am afraid," but rather, "When I am afraid." There are times when we find ourselves during a storm, either within ourselves or in our outward circumstances. At first, we're afraid. But when we consider our option, we can turn from fear to faith.

As these disciples learned to do, so we learn to place our faith in the Savior who is there for us. As David said, "Therefore we will not fear, though the earth should change, though the mountains shake in the heart of the sea; (Psalm 46:2). God is with us, even when health fails, a loved one dies, a job is lost or a child rebels.

As the old gospel song puts it,

> "No waters can swallow the ship where lies,
> The Master of ocean, and earth and skies."

My son, Kyle, as a young boy was obsessed with monsters. When I would put him to bed, I'd do a ritual of chasing all monsters on the loose into his closet, shutting the door and commanding them to stay put for the night. Kyle thought I was bigger and stronger than any monster. If we but realized our God is bigger and stronger than any storm, that he's with us, our fear would become faith. He's bigger than our enemy nations, and he's bigger than whatever threatens you.

It's interesting that Jesus was asleep in the stern of the boat. He knew the storm was coming even as he fell asleep. Though asleep, he was still in control. What a vivid picture of the Master so in control of things that he can sleep! But the Father wasn't asleep. The Son trusted the Father completely and perfectly. Jesus knew that his heavenly Father was watching over him and his disciples, even though they were in a state of panic. The Son had inspired David to write in his psalm,

> *"He will not let your foot be moved;*
> *he who keeps you will not slumber.*

> *He who keeps Israel*
> *will neither slumber nor sleep."* (Psalm 121:3-4).

Luke's account of this event has the disciples calling Jesus "Master" (8:24). They realized they were in great danger and went to Jesus and woke him saying, "Master, Master, we're going to drown!" "Master" is the same word that was used for ship captains.

Henry Blackaby grew up near the Pacific Coast in Canada, just south of Alaska. He was told by sailors that the time to get scared in a storm at sea is when the captain gets scared. If he is calm, you can afford to be calm.

You'll never find Jesus in a panic because he's the Master, the Captain. He could trust himself and his disciples to the God who was watching over him. He inspired also these words of David:

> *"I will both lie down and sleep in peace;*
> *for you alone, O LORD, make me lie down in safety."* (Psalm 4:8).

The disciples were amazed not only that Jesus could sleep in the storm, but also were dismayed that he didn't seem to care that they might drown. The disciples were rude to Jesus, to say the least. They awakened him and demanded, "Don't you care if we drown?" "Jesus, you're supposed to be in charge here, and are supposed to be keeping us away from storms. You're not being much of a leader," seemed to be what they were saying to Jesus.

That may be what we're saying about our storms going on right now. "Lord, you are supposed to at least show me that you care, even if you're not able to keep me clear of the storms. But it seems you don't care that I'm drowning in my problems right now."

The truth is that Jesus is with us, and he cares, and he can calm the storms. He also could have led us away from the storms, but he's more interested in our trusting him than in our being out of trouble. When our hearts are gripped with fear, it's difficult to be calm and in a sense of panic we may cry out rudely to God, something like, "Don't you care that I'm possibly going to lose my job? Or my health or my spouse' health? Or my marriage? Or my family?"

The Psalms are a great prayer and praise book that tells us it's OK to cry out to God, to raise a lament and even a complaint. God wants us to cry to him, even in our panic, fear, unbelief, or anger. But if we stand before this great God, we'll soon begin to realize his great patience with us based on his great love for us.

God loves us and accepts our fears that lead us to him. Then, as we, like the disciples, confess our unbelief in our cries of panic, he helps us to love and trust him. As he reveals himself in power and grace, we learn to place calm faith in him.

Faith is the gift that enables us to see things from God's point of view. When we can see the truth as it is in Jesus, we have a different perspective on life's storms. When we can see Jesus amidst life's storms, we are able to see his loving control of all things. Often, in our fear of the storm, we leave Jesus out of this simple equation: "The storm plus Jesus equals deliverance."

When Jesus is present, fear is illogical. The disciples cried out that they were going to drown. Was that logical? No, because Jesus was with them. The presence of Jesus changes the truth about our circumstances. Jesus had promised them that they were going to the other side of the lake. Jesus' commandments are always his enablements. He didn't promise an easy trip, but he did give a guaranteed arrival (Wiersbe). My need and challenge are to practice the presence of Jesus.

That's exactly why Paul was unafraid when he was arrested, and his life was in danger. The Lord had assured him that his mission and life's purpose was not yet over (Acts 23:11). When he was on board the ship to Rome, and a fierce storm threatened him and the other passengers, the Lord assured Paul that they would survive the storm because God's purpose was that he preaches the gospel in Rome (Acts 27:23f).

You and I need to remember that our lives are indestructible until he is finished with our task in this mortal life. His will for us can't be frustrated by any threatening storms. When Jesus calmed the storm with a word, the disciples responded with awe. When Jesus calms our storms, we have a right kind of fear of him.

As a child, I stood in awe of my daddy and feared his discipline. Yet I never doubted his love for me. We can and must both fear and love God, and as we stand before him we realize we need fear nothing or no one else. Faith in God is a decision, and he is patient with us as we learn to fear him and trust in him.

The calming of this storm caused the disciples to worship the Lord Jesus in reverence and awe, and likely it led them to greater trust in him. Isn't it good news that we don't have to fear any approaching storm? I like the psalmist's words that the righteous person has no fear of bad news (Psalm 112:7). Storms are sure to come. Maybe you've seen the worst of them, and perhaps you haven't. We all face the last enemy, death. Our Lord Jesus is the Master of the storms.

CH Spurgeon said, "Fair weather faith is really no faith." Faith is trusting God in life's storms and through uncertain days.

Maybe as believers we've been practical atheists, living as though God doesn't exist. I remind you my fellow believers that we're called to be the Good Ship Dale Heights. It's not perfect, but Jesus is with us in the boat, and he's given us a task, our mission. I recall seeing fishing boats in the Holy Land, in a museum by the Lake of Galilee. They were rough, quite small little vessels, and no match for a furious storm. And Dale Heights Church is no match for the storms either. We must as never before put our total dependence and trust in Jesus, the Master of the wind and waves.

As I look at this living parable, I ask, "What is Jesus teaching me? How does he want me to join in this narrative?" I know he doesn't want me to doubt his wisdom, power and love in my life. This doubt is why Jesus rebuked the panicked disciples. They had doubted that he would or could save them from the storm and that he cared for them. But he expected them to awaken him and implore him to act, even as I desperately tried to practice his presence in the wee hours this morning. I'm glad he invites us to come to him, to rouse him and say, "Master, Lord Jesus, deliver me!"

# Service: the Jesus Way to Greatness

## Mark 10:35-45

> *35 James and John, the sons of Zebedee, came forward to him and said to him, "Teacher, we want you to do for us whatever we ask of you." 36 And he said to them, "What is it you want me to do for you?" 37 And they said to him, "Grant us to sit, one at your right hand and one at your left, in your glory." 38 But Jesus said to them, "You do not know what you are asking. Are you able to drink the cup that I drink or be baptized with the baptism that I am baptized with?" 39 They replied, "We are able." Then Jesus said to them, "The cup that I drink you will drink; and with the baptism with which I am baptized, you will be baptized; 40 but to sit at my right hand or at my left is not mine to grant, but it is for those for whom it has been prepared."*
>
> *41 When the ten heard this, they began to be angry with James and John. 42 So Jesus called them and said to them, "You know that among the Gentiles those whom they recognize as their ruler's lord it over them, and their great ones are tyrants over them. 43 But it is not so among you; but whoever wishes to become great among you must be your servant, 44 and whoever wishes to be first among you must be slave of all. 45 For the Son of Man came not to be served but to serve, and to give his life a ransom for many."*

James and John, the sons of Zebedee, came to Jesus asking a favor. They assumed, by ignoring or misunderstanding what Jesus had taught them earlier about greatness through humble service, that prestigious positions in the coming kingdom of God were now open to the first applicants. They still, despite what Jesus had been saying about the nature of his kingdom, that they were about to become part of a radically new political kingdom, over which Jesus would reign triumphant over their enemies, including the occupying Roman forces. Thus, James and John wanted to be first to ask Jesus to give them a place on his right hand, as second in command of the kingdom, and on his left, as second in command. Matthew's account tells us that their mother was their intermediary, asking this favor for her sons, James and John. Like any good mother, she wanted what was best for her boys (Matt. 20:20-21); and how proud she would have been to have had her sons in positions of importance!

I'm reminded of the lady who bragged to her friends about her son's important new job that put him over some 500 people. Little did her friends know that her son's job was mowing the grass in a 500-grave cemetery! In the eyes of God, the work of a gardener is no lower than that of a company executive and to him a gardener can be a greater person than a head of state. But even as followers of Christ we often love what the fallen world loves, such as "the lust of the eyes and the boasting of what [we have and do]" (1 Jn. 2:15-17).

James and John were evidencing the influence of the surrounding culture upon their thinking and ambition. Greco-Roman culture despised the characteristic of humility, which was not considered a virtue but rather a weakness. Like the culture around them, these brothers were ambitious to have positions of power, prestige and worldly importance (e.g.v.42).

Ironically, as the disciples followed Jesus toward his cross, they seemed to become more infected with this worldly idea of greatness and the ambition for success as the world views it. Earlier they had argued about "who was the greatest." And so, patiently and lovingly, Jesus sat down, called the twelve and said, "If anyone wants to be first, he must be the very last, and the servant of all" (9:33-35). Obviously, they hadn't learned very well, because we find them once again seeking places of prominence, where they would be regarded as great in the eyes of others. After Jesus' reminder of his looming execution and resurrection, still they were obsessed with their personal ambition.

This worldly desire for power, prestige and control over others has been a problem in the kingdom since these first disciples and the first century church. James calls the kind of "wisdom" that is based on pride "devilish" (Jas. 3:15). He notes that those in the church who "harbor bitter envy and selfish ambition" in their hearts are thinking like the fallen world and even the devil himself. And he notes that "where you have envy and selfish ambition, there you find disorder and every evil practice" (Jas. 3:13-18). The spiritual health and unity of any church or organization is always ruined by the envy and selfish ambition of those who have failed to understand the heart of Christ, which is one of humble service and of preferring one another in love. The worst kind of power struggles often are those in a church, where people often live out their personal ambitions and desires for power and control, usually when they feel powerless and unsuccessful in their jobs or marriages.

But then the Gospel clearly says that the way to this final and future glory is the way of the cross. Jesus had to suffer and die for us as a prelude to his glory in heaven and his everlasting reign. And we also must take the way of the cross, our cross of weakness, self-denial and obedience to Christ and willingness to suffer for the sake of his name. Thus, Jesus told James and John they really did not understand what they were asking (v.38). He then asked if they were able to drink his cup and share his baptism (v.38). The cup represented the cup of the wrath of God against sin. Jesus would have to drink that cup of suffering in his crucifixion. He would bear the sin of the world. His baptism and theirs would be total immersion in a life of tribulation. Thus, Jesus asked if James and John were ready to follow him in a life of suffering and self-denial.

Although they glibly replied that they were able to share his suffering, Jesus replied that indeed they would suffer. James would become, as we see in the Book of Acts, the first of the disciples to be martyred (12:2). John was tortured and exiled to the Isle of Patmos in AD 95. But also, Jesus said that the places of special honor would be conferred by the heavenly Father, in the right time and way. Perhaps Jesus was implying that the Father would confer everlasting glory in the consummated kingdom upon those who were focused on the way of the cross, who were faithfully living a cruciform life of self-denial and obedience witness and service to the glory of Christ. Jesus noted that the Father knows who the faithful ones are.

Christ Jesus, the eternal Son of God, entered this sinful, needy world to rescue us. Jesus served us by being our ransom sacrifice. He gave his life to purchase our liberation from bondage to sin, death and condemnation. Jesus employed the language of one who purchases the freedom of another who has been condemned to a life of slavery.

Jesus says that he did not come to be served. There is nothing we can do to deserve or to earn this pardon and forgiveness we so desperately need. We can't "serve" him by our merits, efforts, or knowledge. All we can do is admit our need. Even faith, the faith to believe in Jesus and to turn from sin to trust in God, is the gift of God. "*It* is the gift of God (Eph. 2:8-9). Jesus gave his life to ransom us from our bondage to sin and death and has ransomed us to a life of serving.

We, the ransomed, are indeed no longer our own. We belong to Christ the Ransom-payer. The final verse in our text is a "how-much-more" argument: "For *even the Son of Man* did not come to be served, but to serve, and to give his life a ransom for many." Jesus is saying, "If I came to serve you, how much more should you, my ransomed people, live to serve others!"

Demosthenes, the 3rd Century BC Athenian orator and statesman, noted that the law decreed that one who is ransomed becomes the property of the one who paid the ransom. And Paul the Apostle echoes this thought when he writes that we who are ransomed are no longer our own. We "were bought with a price" (1 Cor. 6:19). Although we are ransomed by grace alone, that grace is not cheap. It wasn't cheap for Jesus and it isn't for us either. It costs us our self-centered lives. Now we belong to Jesus and we are accountable to follow him as Lord and to join him in his service to the world. We're not autonomous servants, "doing our own thing" for God; rather, we're servants of God, serving alongside Jesus and his people.

Just before his Last Supper with his disciples, Jesus washed his disciples' feet, giving a dramatic portrait of servant-hood. Traditionally the servant washed his master's feet, but in this instance, Jesus reversed the roles and took a towel and a basin of water and washed the feet of his disciples, demonstrating the truth of our text, that indeed he had come to serve us as Savior and supreme Servant. But also, Jesus washed the feet of the disciples to give them and us an example of the attitude we must have toward one another (Jn. 13:1-17).

It doesn't come naturally for us to serve others in humility. As we've noted, it's a very cross-cultural, yea, anti-cultural thing to do. And sometimes it's even at odds with "church thinking." What we need is the attitude of Christ. For this reason, Paul upheld Jesus' example of service to the church in Philippi, which was disturbed by divisiveness, selfish ambition and vain conceit, with all looking after their own interests (Phil. 2:3f). As a corrective to this worldly thinking in the church Paul exhorted the Philippian believers to have the same attitude as that of Christ Jesus, writing or quoting a hymn, saying that Christ Jesus…

> *who, though he was in the form of God,*
> *did not regard equality with God*
> *as something to be exploited,*
> *7 but emptied himself,*
> *taking the form of a slave,*
> *being born in human likeness.*
> *And being found in human form,*
> *8 he humbled himself*
> *and became obedient to the point of death—*
> *even death on a cross.* (Phil. 2:6-8)

There's the fallen worldly type of greatness we as believers must eschew. But there's a kingdom greatness to which we may aspire. This idea of kingdom greatness may be what Jesus referred to when he said that "the one who is least in the kingdom of God is greater than he, i.e. John the Baptist (Lk. 7:28). In the kingdom of God, we now participate in the "greater" work of the Holy Spirit, doing greater things than were done during Jesus' earthly ministry (Jn. 14:12). We're now part of his great work of the Spirit, with a servant attitude, which is true kingdom greatness in the eyes of God. It's a call to kingdom of God significance rather than to worldly or even churchly success.

I was moved by reading Mother Teresa's *Come Be My Light: The Private Writings of the "Saint of Calcutta."* What was so impressive was her consistent commitment to honor Jesus through of life of radical obedience. She had vowed to never withhold anything Jesus might ask and to always willingly receive whatever he gives, including serving him in the darkest places of the poorest of India's poor. What spoke so powerfully was her focus on loving and obeying Jesus, even when she experienced deep emotional loneliness and spiritual darkness. She identified her experiences with the suffering of Jesus and vicariously experienced Jesus' "thirst for souls." What resulted from the life of Mother Teresa is a legacy of a life lived in service to others and deep, abiding love for Jesus, regardless of the apparent void of the sense of Jesus' love for her. She was consumed with an obsession that she was living out Jesus' teaching that to minister to the sick, lonely and dying was to minister to Jesus himself (Matt. 25:31-46). What God was doing all along through Teresa's simple life of obedience was shaping in her life a close replication of the character of Jesus' own greatness.

Jesus says we too can achieve greatness through service. He uses the words *diakonos* and *doulos*, servant and slave, to describe our calling. A servant was one called to do ordinary and humble tasks, such as waiting on tables. The truly great Christian is one who does what needs to be done to encourage others and to demonstrate love. The great servant gives with no thought for recognition. A slave is one who belongs to his or her master and is totally answerable to and dependent upon the master. A Christian "slave" is totally dependent on Jesus and has no life except for Christ and his glory.

Jesus came to be our servant, to do what we desperately need but could never provide for ourselves. We can't add to or improve on his ministry to us. All we can do is humbly receive Jesus as our Servant Savior and trust him alone for our salvation ransom. But receiving his salvation gift means we become his servants and slaves. There can be immediate results, such as when you turn off your favorite TV program or sports event and do something, even if it's an onerous task, for your spouse. My guess is you'll get more satisfaction from your spouse's gratitude than from seeing your favorite team score the winning touchdown! Opportunities to serve are all around us.

I want to be a more faithful pastor, serving a faithful people, who serve one another out of love for Jesus, our Servant Example.

# Jesus Expects Fruit

## Mark 11:12-14; 20-25

*12 On the following day, when they came from Bethany, he was hungry. 13 Seeing in the distance a fig tree in leaf, he went to see whether perhaps he would find anything on it. When he came to it, he found nothing but leaves, for it was not the season for figs. 14 He said to it, "May no one ever eat fruit from you again." And his disciples heard it.*

*20 In the morning as they passed by, they saw the fig tree withered away to its roots. 21 Then Peter remembered and said to him, "Rabbi, look! The fig tree that you cursed has withered." 22 Jesus answered them, "Have faith in God. 23 Truly I tell you, if you say to this mountain, 'Be taken up and thrown into the sea,' and if you do not doubt in your heart but believe that what you say will come to pass, it will be done for you. 24 So I tell you, whatever you ask for in prayer, believe that you have received it, and it will be yours.*

*25 "Whenever you stand praying, forgive, if you have anything against anyone; so that your Father in heaven may also forgive you your trespasses."*

It's been noted that the cursing of the fig tree is the only purely destructive action on the part of Jesus throughout his earthly ministry. He afterward purged the temple, but that was an action with a positive and corrective purpose. He destroyed the herd of swine, but only to rid the Gerasene man of demons (Mk. 5:1-20). One scholar labeled Jesus' action as petulant and selfish (W Barclay), but such interpreters miss the point. Jesus, the eternal Son of God and Co-Creator, has the right to create a fig tree to illustrate a truth. Since we think nothing of cutting down perfectly good pine trees to symbolize Christmas, we should understand Jesus' curse on the fig tree as a perfectly legitimate way of symbolizing his judgment on Israel, who had failed to be a people bringing God glory as a light to the nations. Because of this failure God's judgment came upon them (Is. 5:1-7). Jesus is still concerned about the fruitfulness of his people. It's the impact of our lives that honors him.

As with all texts that I preach, I'm forced to let the text speak to me first. What does this text say about my impact for the kingdom? What does it mean for me to be a fruitful Christian and an effective servant leader as pastor of this church? What does it look like for you to be impactful and effective? And, what does it mean for Dale Heights to be a fruitful church? I submit that all our lives must be open to Jesus' inspection.

It's interesting and at first bewildering to note the response of Jesus to the fruitlessness of the fig tree. The time of the year, Passover, was probably April, and not the season for figs to be in fruit, as Mark says (13). Although the reaction of Jesus appears unreasonable and petulant, it was calculated. Jesus demonstrated that he has the right to expect fruit all the time. What's impossible in nature, the bearing of fruit out of season, he expects in the spiritual and Kingdom of God realm. Paul admonished young Timothy to be prepared and useful (in fruitful service) both "in season and out of season" (NIV 2 Tim. 4:2). God inspects and expects from the believer results from start to finish. There's no time in our lives when we're immune from Jesus' expectations of us. In that sense we're never on holiday.

Jesus expects to see fruit, i.e., evidence of genuine conversion. He expects, and he inspects, and he judges us based on the evidence of a changed and changing life. By grace through the cross we're being saved to a life of following Jesus as Lord. And by grace alone are we truly converted. In the Sermon on the Mount, Jesus described the kind of life that is produced by faith. It's a life of true love and righteousness, not just outward legal observances. And Jesus ended that sermon by saying God will judge by the fruit of our lives, and not by our empty words (Matt. 7:15-23)

The fruit Jesus expects is a life that is grace-saved and grace-enabled to reflect his character. Jesus came to save us from the guilt of sin, but also from the power of sin. He enables us, not to live sinlessly perfect lives on earth, but progressively Christ-like lives of love and obedience. He's looking for the fruit of the Holy

Spirit in our lives (1 Cor. 13; Gal. 5:22-23). He expects growth, not perfection (2 Pet. 1:8). God wants a deepening love relationship with us. When we live by the assurance of his love for us, we're able to love him and others. Love is the fruit he desires.

Unbelievers will be judged not because of their "decisions" only, but because they refused the gift of his forgiveness and love. Jesus judged the temple, which was to be literally and finally destroyed by the Romans in AD 70, because of it had lost its purpose. The purpose of the temple was to be a gathering place of all peoples to worship, express love and to glorify God. Therefore, unbelievers are judged, because of their failure to fulfill their purpose in creation, which is to worship and glorify God forever.

Jesus is inspecting our lives and the impact they have on others. God has the perfect right to be pleased with us and honored through our lives. And that means that God's love flows through our lives to others in a way that points them to Christ. The obstacle to a fruitful life is a mountain that God alone can move (23). To the Hebrews a mountain symbolized a great difficulty, and a human impossibility. What are the mountains in our lives that are keeping us from being fruitful? Our becoming fruitful has nothing to do with our faith or our prayers or our work. Apart from the grace of God there's no fruit. Faith is simply our response of trust in and surrender to Almighty God who allows us to link up with him. Faith is to live in the awareness of God's love.

To understand Jesus' promise of answered prayer (22-24), we must consider the larger context of all his teachings on prayer. Jesus teaches us to pray in his name, which means we ask for those things Jesus himself would ask of the Father (Jn.14:13). The key to knowing what's in his will and name, is for us to have a relationship of "remaining" in him, as a branch remains in the vine. "If you remain in me and my words remain in you, ask whatever you wish, and it will be given you" (Jn. 15:7). And only as we grow in a personal relationship with Jesus can we begin to discern what he wants for us.

Like you, I've asked God for things that didn't seem all that bad. In fact, I thought they might just be what he would want for me. But as I took these matters to the Lord in regular prayer, my desires began to shift away from what I thought God wanted for me toward his perfect, and much better, will for me. Effective praying leads us to the mind and heart of God, which is praying in Jesus' name, asking what he wants (..." the Father will give you whatever you ask in my name" (Jn. 15:16)

As we have a love relationship with Jesus Christ and abide in him as a branch in the vine, as Jesus says, we obey him and walk with him as his friends, and then bear fruit for his glory. Jesus was hungry when he approached the tree, but his hunger didn't cause him to act precipitously, capriciously, or selfishly. Nor was Jesus desperately hungry in a physical sense. After all, he had fasted once for 40 days and nights. And because Jesus had been staying in the home of Mary and Martha in near-by Bethany, we probably had been served breakfast. His "hunger" in this instance was expressive of his hunger that he be glorified by our fruitfulness. Jesus has a great yearning that we glorify him by the fruitfulness of godly, prayerful and faithful living. But I think also that Jesus hungers for a vital love relationship with us that truly delights his heart as well as ours. Prayer is to be primarily a love relationship with God.

As Jesus, in our text, encourages the disciples to bear fruit for his glory, he says, "Therefore, I tell you, whatever you ask for in prayer, believe that you have received it, and it will be yours" (24). Prayer is required for growth in faith, which is essential for the kind of praying that God honors. We may begin with weak prayers and weak faith, but all that is needed is a great God. He'll strengthen our faith as we look to Jesus and trust and live in his presence. Prayer then becomes more than the time on our knees or seated in our prayer closet. Prayer becomes a part of our day, as we pray throughout the day. We even learn to turn our life into a prayer, desiring what God desires.

The Bible doesn't get too specific about the mechanics of prayer. Jesus gave a model to us (Matt. 6:9-13), which tells us to pray as an act of worship and submission to the Father, and for Kingdom priorities, trusting God to meet our other needs. Posture is not important, nor is formality or length. Pray is the upward turning of the heart. It is to be shaped around the word and is an upward turning of the heart to God. As we pray for one another, we're to seek God's grace to remind us of our dependence on him and are to live in thankfulness to him. Sometimes the most appropriate prayer is simply, "Help!"

Jesus says prayer must be out of our relationship with him, but also with a right relationship with others. Jesus says, *"Whenever you stand praying, forgive, if you have anything against anyone; so that your Father in heaven may also forgive you your trespasses"* (25). We can't pray for each other if we're out of sorts with one another. And, that goes for our relationships with all in the Body of Christ. We must first be reconciled—forgiven and forgiving toward all if we are to have answered prayers. That also means, as Peter reminds us, that we must have a right relationship with our spouse if we are to be effective in our praying (1 Pet. 3:7).

Jesus said that he chose and appointed us to "go and bear fruit—fruit that will last" (Jn. 15:16). This is the fruit of love and all the fruit of the Spirit (Gal. 5:22-23). We might not be allowed to see the fruit and effectiveness of our life and witness in this life, but God sees and remembers. All of us need to examine ourselves to ask if we are bearing fruit that gives evidence of true conversion. Is God being glorified through my life? He didn't redeem us primarily for us to escape hell. He saved us through the blood of Christ that we might live for his pleasure and honor.

Today I'm asking God to show me what my life should look like to pass his fruit inspection. By his grace alone can I be saved from the judgment of unfruitfulness, despite my best efforts. I wonder how my life and ministry through all these years measure up to God's fruit inspection. I must ask God to come into the temple of my heart and drive out any corruption, self-centeredness and neglect of true prayer and worship. I must ask him to prune from my life anything that makes me less than fruitful and productive in his kingdom.

Jan showed me a cartoon sent to her by a friend, that pictured Billy Graham having arrived at the gate of heaven, greeted perhaps by St. Peter. Inside the gate, a multitude of people stood waiting to receive the great evangelist, and St. Peter explains to Billy, "These people all want to thank you." Obviously, these were meant to picture the multitudes that made decisions for Christ during his world-wide preaching ministry.

The life of Billy Graham and his evangelistic ministry were phenomenal, and certainly his life and work were fruitful. But I happen to believe that your life in the eyes of God can have equal significance and bring great glory to him. Who knows whose life is the most fruitful? It might have something to do with the measure of our love for God and our trust in him and how we let him love us. We need to know he likes us, and to no longer think his love is conditional upon our performance and what others can measure. Maybe there are people who struggle with doubt or with personal problems, but who please God by reflecting his grace and forgiveness. Even those who struggle to the end with addiction but learn to pray and love and trust. Maybe the one who enters eternity with more glory than Billy Graham will be a forgotten prisoner in North Korea who has never failed to cry to God for his deliverance for her fellow sufferers.

I've been taking a lot of self-inventory in recent days, and today's Scripture has led me to the 92nd Psalm: "The righteous will flourish like a palm tree, they will grow like a cedar of Lebanon; planted in the house of the Lord, they will flourish in the courts of our God. *They will still bear fruit in old age*, they will stay fresh and green, proclaiming, 'The Lord is upright; he is my Rock, and there is no wickedness in him" (vv. 12-14).

Lord, make me fruitful. Make *us* fruitful.

# Waiting Orders

## Luke 24:36-49

*³⁶ While they were talking about this, Jesus himself stood among them and said to them, "Peace be with you." ³⁷ They were startled and terrified and thought that they were seeing a ghost. ³⁸ He said to them, "Why are you frightened, and why do doubts arise in your hearts? ³⁹ Look at my hands and my feet; see that it is I myself. Touch me and see; for a ghost does not have flesh and bones as you see that I have." ⁴⁰ And when he had said this, he showed them his hands and his feet. ⁴¹ While in their joy they were disbelieving and still wondering, he said to them, "Have you anything here to eat?" ⁴² They gave him a piece of broiled fish, ⁴³ and he took it and ate in their presence.*

*⁴⁴ Then he said to them, "These are my words that I spoke to you while I was still with you—that everything written about me in the law of Moses, the prophets, and the psalms must be fulfilled." ⁴⁵ Then he opened their minds to understand the scriptures, ⁴⁶ and he said to them, "Thus it is written, that the Messiah is to suffer and to rise from the dead on the third day, ⁴⁷ and that repentance and forgiveness of sins is to be proclaimed in his name to all nations, beginning from Jerusalem. ⁴⁸ You are witnesses of these things. ⁴⁹ And see, I am sending upon you what my Father promised; so, stay here in the city until you have been clothed with power from on high."*

We're familiar with marching orders that are sometimes given to a military unit, with instructions for following a strategy for a combat mission. To go at the right time can be the difference between victory and defeat. But the risen Jesus appeared to his disciples to give them *waiting orders*, to stay in the city until they would be clothed with power from on high (49).

Since these words of Jesus and the coming of the Spirit on the Day of Pentecost 2000 years ago, the Spirit has come and has been doing his mighty kingdom work. And those of us who are followers of Jesus realize we received the Spirit of God when we first believed in Jesus. And perhaps we've also come to understand that as followers of Jesus we need the baptism of the fullness of the Holy Spirit to live for and serve Jesus well. What's certain is that we all need to learn to "stay for the Spirit," whether for the first time as a new Christian or, as in the case of us older followers of Jesus, as a pattern of living.

That verb "to stay" means literally "to sit" or "to remain" for a specific purpose. As a long-time follower of Jesus, I'm just now learning that the risen Jesus wants me to stay until his blessings become a part of my daily experience.

Jesus appeared to his disciples to make unmistakably clear that he'd been raised bodily from death and the grave. He was no phantom of their imagination nor a shadowy ghost. Jesus' resurrection body was a physical, even if a trans-physical body, capable of exceeding our present bodily limitations but just as real as our earthly bodies. Jesus presented himself for the disciples' examination and even ate a piece of fish to display his real, physical presence.

Jesus greeted the disciples with "Peace be with you." "Shalom," or peace, is more than the absence of conflict or war. The peace that the risen Jesus brings is a right relationship with God, the healing of forgiveness of sin and the removal of guilt, and the health and wholeness of mind and spirit under the renewing grace of God. The risen Jesus gave the disciples the blessing of eternal and abundant life, a life lived in peace with God and aligned with his kingdom purposes.

If we stay for the Spirit, we'll realize that Jesus lives and his kingdom is among us and even within us. We'll realize the risen Jesus reigns over this world and over the circumstances of our lives, and that we're a part of his kingdom coming to fulfillment on this earth. To know that Jesus' is physically raised tells us that the kingdom of God is not "otherworldly" but has invaded and is transforming this physical, tangible, yet fallen world. It's to know that these bodies of ours are, though decaying and wasting away, will be transformed and fitted for eternity. Thus, we treat them as Spirit-inhabited temples of God. And we regard the creation and, yes, the suffering environment as created and soon-to-be redeemed as the new heaven and earth, and we thus treat it with care and respect. And we view everyone as a creature with an everlasting destiny of being like Jesus or like the devil himself.

Jesus gives the disciples in the Upper Room an unforgettable Bible study. When we stay for the Spirit and let the risen Jesus teach us from his word, we can't be mere academics with Scripture, endlessly debating obscure and/or controversial passages. We'll understand that the Bible comes alive by the Holy Spirit as the voice of God to us. Jesus reminded the disciples that the word of God will be fulfilled in every part, from the first prophecies of Genesis to the last ones of Revelation (44).

It's the risen Jesus, through the Holy Spirit, who opens our minds to understand the truth of the word. Jesus "opened their minds so that they could understand the Scriptures" (45). Apart from the Spirit of God, writes Paul, we cannot understand spiritual truth (1 Cor. 2:14). Even as regenerated children of God who have the Spirit, we can't read the Bible as though it were dead history or propositional truth for others. We must read it with a spirit of expectancy, praying to the Spirit of God to open our eyes to show us the wonderful truths God has for us (Ps. 119:18). So, we must stay for the Spirit.

In my personal walk with God, the word is essential to guide, guard and encourage me (Ps. 119:105). And in my darkest hours I've found the essential encouragement of Scripture that always gives me hope (Rom. 15:4). It's essential that we have frequent time alone with the risen Lord Jesus. His word comes often through Scripture but also from unexpected sources.

This past week, after parking my car at the fitness center where I was headed for a workout, a young mom was assisting her children out of her car. She yelled a warning to her little boy, who was headed unsupervised away from the car, "Stay right there!" she commanded, and then took his hand as she led her kids toward the child care center. It was as if the Lord told me to stay, to be certain I was holding his hand before I plunged into my encounters, with potential for good or ill. And sure enough, in just a moment I encountered an irritating situation when I was tempted to returned rudeness with rudeness.

When we listen to Jesus speak from the word, his word to us, it's always about following him in the awareness of his presence and our constant dependence on him to guide our conversations and guard our spirits. And the only way we can follow him and be of use to him is through our cross, a cruciform life of dying to self-centered self and losing our lives in his (Matt. 10:38f). When Jesus speaks to us he always gives the invitation, in the words of Dietrich Bonhoeffer, to "come and die." Therefore, the Bible is not a dead text for the curious, but rather a dangerous text for the complacent and a new way of living for the serious disciples of Jesus.

We must stay for the Spirit, who's the key to everything we need for life and eternity. He's the one who is "God with us" and God within us now that the risen Jesus is ascended to heaven. He is the one who transforms us into the children of God and makes us day by day into a greater likeness of Jesus himself (2 Corinthians 3:18). The presence of the Spirit in us is the key to every blessing. We have every right and reason to keep on asking, seeking and knocking before the throne of grace because we are seeking, not selfish little things for ourselves, but for the life of God, the fullness of the Holy Spirit himself, who is the source of everything else we need.

All the disciples knew that, having faltered in their faith, fled from the scene of Jesus' execution, and even having denied him, they needed something to happen in them to do the work he had commissioned them to do. When we take Scripture seriously, and Jesus teaches us in our time of listening prayer, we realize just how much we need, yes depend on the Holy Spirit.

As someone has remarked, sometimes the most eloquent prayer we can offer is "Help me, Jesus!" And therefore, we're to stay for the Spirit. Think of Peter's miserable failure in his three-fold denial of the Lord here in Luke's gospel. But in Volume Two, Acts, Peter is the courageous, indomitable witness, preacher and leader of the church militant and triumphant. The character change in all the disciples is due to the staying for the Spirit, who would clothe them with power from on high (49).

When we turn our lives to Jesus Christ, we immediately receive the Holy Spirit. But we must learn what it means to be baptized in the Holy Spirit, who demands complete control of our lives. To live in obedience to the word and to honor Jesus Christ are the conditions for being filled with the Holy Spirit. And throughout our lives and as a daily practice we must stay for the Spirit. That means that after my time of listening prayer I need to stay still before the risen Lord Jesus and ask him to cover me, to clothe me with his Spirit. I must ask him to make me mindful of the promise, principle and direction he gave to me from his word during my listening prayer. Only after my life is centered in the risen Jesus and I am filled with his Spirit and under the authority of his word am I ready to face the world, the flesh and the devil.

Throughout the day, at times I must stop before making that phone call or writing that sermon or entering that meeting or sanctuary. I must stop and wait for the Spirit, for the risen Jesus, to guide me, protect me and empower me as his servant, witness and messenger. You too need to learn to just stop throughout the day and for a few moments do nothing but stay. Pray and wait for the assurance that Jesus is alive and within you. Stay for the word to be clear to you once again as you make that your prayer. Stay for the Spirit while you are waiting for the computer to power up; when waiting at a stoplight; or for your turn in the doctor's office.

When we learn to stay for the Spirit we have a joy-inducing awareness of the risen Lord. As David wrote and sang, "You will fill me with joy in your presence" (Ps. 16:11). We must stay for the Spirit to find the joy that comes with his presence and from his Word conveyed to our hearts by the Spirit. The believer's joy is not dependent on circumstances, as is happiness. Our joy is a discipline, or at least it comes from the discipline of our personal and corporate worship. When we focus on Jesus he gives us his peace and assurance of his love and grace. The result is joy, that sense of well-being, of spiritual wholeness and health as was announced by the risen Lord Jesus (36).

Like these disciples, when we stay for the Spirit we'll become worshipers and as we live in the fullness of the Spirit, we'll be joyful worshipers, who praise God, delighting him and finding our joy and delight in him (52). If you find worship a joyless experience, then you desperately need to stay for the Spirit.

For you, to stay for the Spirit may be to first come to faith in Jesus as Savior and follow him as Lord. The moment you place your trust in him, turning from a life pattern of sin and self, and beginning a life of obedience, you're born from above, of the Holy Spirit. Now you have the Holy Spirit. Rather, *he has you*. Then ask him to baptize, to anoint you with the fullness of his presence and power, that you might practice his presence, live according to his word, and be his faithful, fruitful and joyful witness.

Begin each day by staying for the Spirit in listening prayer. Before each task and personal encounter remind yourself of God's word to you and realize the presence of the risen Jesus with you, within you. Sometimes the most eloquent and practical prayer we can say is "Help me, Jesus!" This is staying for the Spirit. "Help me to do your will. Help me to express faith through love for this person. Help me through this temptation to emerge a victor through the risen, living Lord Jesus."

No parent would think of letting a small child wander off by herself, unprotected, undirected and undetected. Remember all the times your child ran off ahead of you and you said, "Wait! Stay right where you are!" And then you caught up with your child. God the Father wants to be our protector, guide and keeper, and he wants us to join him in his kingdom work. Our order from the Master is, "Stay for the Spirit!" It's the key to victory.

# Jesus, the True Vine

## John 15:1-11

> *"I am the true vine, and my Father is the vine grower. ² He removes every branch in me that bears no fruit. Every branch that bears fruit he prunes to make it bear more fruit. ³ You have already been cleansed by the word that I have spoken to you. ⁴ Abide in me as I abide in you. Just as the branch cannot bear fruit by itself unless it abides in the vine, neither can you unless you abide in me. ⁵ I am the vine, you are the branches. Those who abide in me and I in them bear much fruit, because apart from me you can do nothing. ⁶ Whoever does not abide in me is thrown away like a branch and withers; such branches are gathered, thrown into the fire, and burned. ⁷ If you abide in me, and my words abide in you, ask for whatever you wish, and it will be done for you. ⁸ My Father is glorified by this, that you bear much fruit and become my disciples. ⁹ As the Father has loved me, so I have loved you; abide in my love. ¹⁰ If you keep my commandments, you will abide in my love, just as I have kept my Father's commandments and abide in his love. I have said these things to you so that my joy may be in you, and that your joy may be complete."*

How I long to understand and to experience what Jesus is saying to me about remaining/abiding in him in such a way that my life will be fruitful and productive for him! As a pastor, I yearn to see the people I serve individually and in our life together as Jesus' body, bear fruit and be productive for his glory.

The 80th Psalm, after speaking of God's judgment on the unfruitful vine, Israel, prophesies about the "son of man" that God has raised up for himself, who'll bring restoration and salvation to Israel (Psalm 80:17-19). Even as Israel was a miserable failure as God's vine, Jesus is the True Vine who will do what Israel failed to do. He'll perfectly obey the Father and will fulfill the mission given him. And, his life will bring forth much fruit to the glory of the Father. The key to our being productive is to abide in Jesus, the True Vine.

Just as God chose Israel to be his vineyard (Psalm 80:8), so has he chosen and called his people to be a part of his new vineyard, that is, to be part of Christ Jesus, the True Vine.

By grace through faith in Jesus we have been cleansed by the word (3). Because we received grace to believe in Jesus as Savior and have repented of sin, the living word, Jesus, has washed us in his blood and made us alive in him. Our sins are forgiven, and we have eternal life in Jesus. We're connected to him in a life-changing relationship. This relationship is one of an organic, living union with Christ. It's not a mechanical matter of an institutional ritual of "jumping through the hoops" of joining a church and doing religious routines that never affect the heart.

Some modern translations of our scripture text use the verb "remain" in place of "abide." But to me abide connotes a close connection, and commitment to stay within a relationship. Some couples simply remain married, even when they no longer love and respect each other. They're going to remain together legally until the kids go off to college, or whatever. But to abide is to share a mutual relationship of dependence and commitment. An abiding relationship is a productive one. Some people decide to remain nominal Christians with occasional church attendance, but it's another thing to abide in Christ, with a life-changing relationship.

Jesus refers to dead branches that never bear any fruit. No doubt an immediate example was Judas Iscariot. He had a superficial identity with Jesus and the other disciples, yet he didn't connect and didn't remain (much less abide), and thus never produced the fruit of righteousness. Jesus speaks of branches dying because they didn't abide in the vine. True, saving grace reveals itself in the believer's perseverance. Those God grafts into his vine will bear the fruit of perseverance.

God has done his part to graft us into Christ, the True Vine. Now we have the responsibility of abiding in him. This speaks of our total dependence on him: "No branch can bear fruit by itself." No branch can even *live* by itself. We depend on God's grace to save us and keep us. We depend on God for life and eternal life. The Christian life is one of dependency, which is not a popular word in our culture of pride and independence. But as believers in and followers of Jesus, we depend on him for life now and a hope for the life to come.

We abide in Christ through faithful praying and prayerful living. Jesus refers to the effective prayers of an abiding life (7). We don't bring him our selfish wish lists, but we come before him to ask what he wants for us. The True Vine's design for our lives also includes the fruit of a godly, holy life. This is the *sine qua non* of the Christian life, that the Holy Spirit produces character that shows we belong to Jesus, that we are new creations (2 Corinthians 5:17).

Jesus says "I am the true vine, and my Father is the gardener. He cuts off every branch in me that bears no fruit, while every branch that does bear fruit he prunes so that it will be even more fruitful" (verse 2). A good vine gardener knows that pruning is best for his crop. And his interest is in the harvest.

The Father is the gardener who continues to prune our lives. One pastor (Kent Hughes) speaks about the "when syndrome," which is our false assumption that someday "when we have grown to maturity in Christ" life will get easier for us. Not true. In my life, the pruning has seemed more severe in my old age. The Gardener never stops pruning us, and pruning usually is uncomfortable, but the heavenly Father's discipline is a sign of his love (Hebrews 12:11). We don't like it, but the Gardener wields his pruning knife. God, the Gardener, is at work to make us like his Son, and he is pruning away every thought, habit, attitude, relationship or possession that keeps us from becoming more like Jesus.

Ridgecrest is a Baptist assembly grounds in the mountains of Western North Carolina, a place very familiar to me. A group of Ridgecrest conferees visited a gift shop in the nearby Town of Black Mountain, watching with amazement a wood carver as he completed work on a beautiful carving of a hound dog. One of the curious tourists asked the woodcarver, "How can you carve from just a block of wood such a beautiful and detailed likeness of a hound dog?" "That's easy, replied the mountain woodcarver, "I just cut away everything that don't look like a hound dog." The divine Gardener just cuts away from our lives and character everything that doesn't look like Jesus.

I've often been encouraged by good friends who've prayed with me during difficult times in recent years, and two of these men made the same statement, unbeknownst to the other: "Lord, I thank you for Roger's troubles." I said to both after their prayers, "That's easy for *you* to say!" I agreed with them. I knew they were thinking about the Scripture that says, "Consider it pure joy, my brothers, whenever you face trials of many kinds, because you know that the testing of your faith develops perseverance. Perseverance must finish its work so that you will be mature and complete, not lacking anything" (James 1:2-4, NIV).

What an amazing truth, that everything the Gardener allows to come our way, he does for our good. And, he always watches over us to see if there's any unproductive, unhealthy growth he needs to cut away. Is there anything that keeps us from loving Jesus and becoming more like him? Even our sense of ease and complacency he may cut away.

O, for grace to enable you and me to say to the Gardener, "You know what I don't. Your perspective is best. "You're perfect in wisdom, power and love. I'll not run from your pruning knife if it will make me more fruitful." We need grace to keep our eyes on the love, wisdom and power of the heavenly Gardener, who has a perfect design for us, for our eternal good and his glory.

The True Vine says as we remain in his love through a prayerful, obedient walk, we'll be blessed with godliness. We cannot always see the fruit of our lives. In fact, the best people will probably be the least aware of the fruit of their godly character since one aspect of the fruit is humility (1 Peter 5:5). Evidently the rogue who wrote the book *Humility and How I Achieved It* missed the whole point and misunderstood the whole concept of humility! As we learn to submit to the heavenly Father's pruning, and even welcome the pruning knife, he grows us in the fruit of maturity in being like Jesus (James 1:2).

His desire also is to bless us with assurance. Jesus says that "This is to my Father's glory, that you bear much fruit, *showing yourselves* (italics mine) to be my disciples" (verse 8). Our assurance that we are God's children is not based on a baptismal certificate or our church membership. It's not even based on a decision we made. Our assurance, according to John's first letter, is based on faith in Jesus Christ as the Son of God and Savior and on the change in our lives that makes us godly and makes us love our brother. And our assurance comes with an awareness of the indwelling Holy Spirit (1 John 3:24). To abide in Christ is to be *at home* with him and to allow him to be at home with us is a deep, personal relationship. Assurance of salvation isn't dependent on emotion, but rather on God's promises and faithfulness expressed in his trustworthy word (2 Timothy 1:12).

Jesus speaks of our relationship with him as one of mutual friendship, and what a gracious gift this is! You know how comfortable you are with a friend. You can freely enter his or her house and pick up where you left off, and you never have to worry about being rejected or condemned for what you say. You can share intimate secrets and receive complete understanding. Even when separated by miles, you stay in touch and let one another know what you're doing (verse 15). Even if you're alone, you're never totally lonely because you have such a friend. And our best Friend, Jesus, never leaves us alone.

Again, although we are saved by grace, we will be judged by our works. Jesus says in Matthew 7:15-20, we will be judged by our fruit, which is the identifying mark of the believer. It is possible for a child of God to wander and become unfruitful and barren, according to 1 Corinthians 3:10-15. Such a Christian will be saved "as one escaping through the fire." His/her works will be lost, as will much of the eternal reward that God can give in heaven. But a Christian who has departed, though not bereft of salvation, is nonetheless without assurance of salvation. The only way to "make your calling and election sure," Peter says is to abound in the virtues that make us effective and productive (2 Peter 1:5-11).

The true vine desires to bless us with joy. Jesus speaks of the need to remain in closest fellowship with his love that we might know his joy (verse 11). There can be joy in Jesus even during those difficult times when he's pruning us.

Someone said when the pruning knife is *in* us the Gardener is closest *to* us. Let us never doubt his love for his children. And in his presence, there's fullness of joy (Psalm 16:11). Joy is so much more than happiness, which depends on felicitous, fortuitous circumstances. Joy is a sense of wellbeing that gives us "gusto," even when we are in seasons of difficulty and pain.

Yet beyond all the above, the True Vine desires to be glorified through us. "My Father is glorified by this, that you bear much fruit and become my disciples," says Jesus (verse 8). God's overarching purpose in all his creation and works of redemption is to glorify himself. He's created all things to reflect his character of holiness and love and has created us and saved us to be his worshipers (John 4:23).

You and I can "do church" without dependence on Jesus, but we can't do kingdom living and work unless we are abiding in the True Vine. I can do pastoral busy work without abiding in Jesus. But I can't preach with anointing, serve with love, and lead to honor Jesus without abiding in the true vine.

I desire my life and our church to be fruitful to the glory of God. But the True Vine, Jesus, desires this more than you or I do. He wants to bless us for his glory. He's able and willing to make us more fruitful than we've ever been. He wants to make a godly, holy people who are seriously following him as Lord. He wants to make us fruitful also in good works, in giving, and in prayerful praise and worship. He wants us to abide in him because he loves us. He even likes us and enjoys us and wants us to enjoy him.

Jesus is the True Vine. Let's abide in him, for his pleasure and glory.

# The Empty Tomb
## John 20:11-18

> *¹¹ But Mary stood weeping outside the tomb. As she wept, she bent over to investigate the tomb; ¹² and she saw two angels in white, sitting where the body of Jesus had been lying, one at the head and the other at the feet. ¹³ They said to her, "Woman, why are you weeping?" She said to them, "They have taken away my Lord, and I do not know where they have laid him." ¹⁴ When she had said this, she turned around and saw Jesus standing there, but she did not know that it was Jesus. ¹⁵ Jesus said to her, "Woman, why are you weeping? Whom are you looking for?" Supposing him to be the gardener, she said to him, "Sir, if you have carried him away, tell me where you have laid him, and I will take him away." ¹⁶ Jesus said to her, "Mary!" She turned and said to him in Hebrew, "Rabbouni!" (which means Teacher). ¹⁷ Jesus said to her, "Do not hold on to me, because I have not yet ascended to the Father. But go to my brothers and say to them, 'I am ascending to my Father and your Father, to my God and your God.'" ¹⁸ Mary Magdalene went and announced to the disciples, "I have seen the Lord"; and she told them that he had said these things to her.*

As much and as often as Jesus told his disciples he would be crucified and raised again, they simply didn't get it. Their understanding of a messiah was rooted in the Jewish expectation of a triumphant king who would overcome all other rulers, political and otherwise, and would immediately inaugurate his kingdom. There was no room for a crucified messiah in their thinking. They believed there would be resurrection in the messianic kingdom, but not that the messiah would suffer and die and be singularly raised from the dead. What Jesus had taught them didn't click in their minds until after they'd seen for themselves evidence of the risen Jesus.

John Updike, captures the convictions of these disciples in his poem, "Seven Stanzas at Easter":

*Make no mistake: if He rose at all*
*it was as His body;*
*if the cells' dissolution did not reverse, the molecules*
*reknit, the amino acids rekindle,*
*the Church will fall.*

*It was not as the flowers,*
*each soft Spring recurrent;*
*it was not as His Spirit in the mouths and fuddled*
*eyes of the eleven apostles;*
*it was as His Flesh: ours.*

*The same hinged thumbs and toes,*
*the same valved heart*
*that — pierced — died, withered, paused, and then*
*regathered out of enduring Might*
*new strength to enclose.*

*Let us not mock God with metaphor,*
*analogy, sidestepping transcendence;*
*making of the event a parable, a sign painted in the*
*faded credulity of earlier ages:*
*let us walk through the door.*

Let's consider the evidence of the empty tomb and what took place in the lives of Mary Magdalene, John and Simon Peter. In the words of John Updike, let's walk through the door.

To the first followers of Jesus, his death meant the loss of hope. When their Lord was arrested and crucified, the disciples had mostly forsaken him and, in Peter's case, had denied him. They were bewildered, frightened, and their hopes were dashed by his death (Luke 24:21). They were so dejected and grief-stricken, they refused to believe the women who reported an empty tomb (Luke 24:22-23). The disciples were grieving over the death of their Lord.

Mary Magdalene was particularly grief-stricken over the death of Jesus. She, from whom Jesus had cast out seven demons, was deeply grateful for all he had done for her and became one of the women who helped to support the disciples (Mk. 16:9; Lk. 8:2-3).

Now that her Lord was dead, and his body likely stolen, what was she to do? Jesus had forgiven her, but how could she know her guilt was removed if her Lord was dead? And then there's Simon Peter, the one who confessed Jesus as "the Christ, the Son of the living God" (Matt. 16:16). He had now denied his Lord three times, exactly as Jesus had predicted (Jn. 18:15-27). His mind must have been swimming with confused thoughts about his master's claims as the great *I Am*, and now he's dead. John, who later wrote this fourth gospel, had paid attention to Jesus' claims, such as "He who has seen me has seen the Father," and "I am the Resurrection and the Life" (Jn. 14:9, 11:25). What do these claims mean now that the great *I Am* is dead?

These disciples had pinned their hopes on Jesus. Now their Lord was dead and gone. The possibility of hope seemed the farthest thing from the minds of Mary, Peter, and John. Mary was so blinded by her tears she could not even see her Lord at first. Without the reality of the resurrection of Jesus, these disciples and all who claim Jesus as Lord are hopeless, embarrassed and pitiable (1 Cor. 15:14-19).

But Mary Magdalene discovered the tomb was empty and ran to tell Peter and John. Their fear was the grave had been robbed. John, the younger, outran the older and probably larger Simon Peter. John stopped at the entrance to the tomb, but Peter, ever impulsive and brazen, walked right in. There lay mysteriously empty grave wrappings. The strips of linen that had been wrapped around Jesus' body were lying as though the body of Jesus had been vaporized (Stott). Peter and John were bewildered by this evidence. Something supernatural had to have happened. The empty cloths were like the chrysalis left by a butterfly.

John simply investigated the tomb at the strips of linen but didn't go in. This was a look of initial surprise and consideration of the evidence. No doubt the idea that something amazing had taken place was in his mind. A lot of people will give the truth of the Gospel an initial look. They, like John, look from the outside. Like John's first glance, some never go beyond a superficial look. And without a thorough look, wrong conclusions are reached, such as

Jesus' being merely a good man and teacher, but certainly not the risen Son of God and Savior of the world.

Simon Peter took a closer look at the evidence of the grave cloths. Again, these strips of linen had simply been vacated and not unraveled. Some here today may be close to faith. The evidence and revelation of Christ and his gospel is in your mind. It's convincing and you have no reason or case for refuting it. But as yet grace has not moved into your heart. John went inside the tomb and "saw and believed." Grace was at work, and he accepted the evidence and within his heart he said "Yes!" to God. He knew Jesus was alive, and right then and there he trusted. It's interesting to note that *"They still did not understand from Scripture that Jesus had to rise from the dead"* (9, NIV). But they had enough evidence to believe Jesus was alive.

Mary had returned to the empty tomb and the angels asked her why she was crying. When she answered that the body of her Lord had been robbed, she turned and saw Jesus. But she didn't recognize him. Jesus' question, "Why are you crying?" was a gentle rebuke. After her remark to Jesus, whom she supposed to be the gardener, he spoke her name. She then turned to him, calling him, "Rabboni," and likely fell at his feet and grasped his ankles. Mary's faith was awakened when she heard the voice of the Good Shepherd, who had said his sheep would hear and follow (Jn. 10:27-28).

A classmate in my seminary pastoral care class expressed his doubt about the historical resurrection of Jesus. Tom had been influenced by the theology of Rudolf Bultmann, the German scholar who set out to de-mythologize Scripture. According to Tom, the historical Resurrection was simply myth and not historic fact. I remember the reply of Professor Wayne Oates, who told this unbelieving student, "The Resurrection is something that has to happen to you." Of course, the Resurrection is a fact of history. We believe in a real Jesus who really died and bodily rose again. Yet, grace is God's initiative that reaches us, and awakens us by the life-giving power of the Holy Spirit. The Resurrection *happens* to you.

The Resurrection happened to Mary, Peter and John. Believers have looked in faith and have experienced the rescuing power of the risen Christ. The Resurrection changed the disciples from defeated adherents into zealous and courageous witnesses in the midst of danger and hostility and unto death by martyrdom. And to this very day, believers are facing persecution and martyrdom because of their indomitable faith in the risen Lord.

Mary had been gratefully devoted to Jesus, but when she saw the risen Lord, her sorrow over his death was turned to joy (Jn. 16:20). Mary held onto Jesus as if to say, "I won't let you be taken from me again!" But Jesus told her about the new way of relating.

Before the cross, the disciples knew Jesus in a mortal way, and were taught, comforted and strengthened by his physical presence. And, as much as Jesus had told them, they simply did not comprehend the necessity of his death or the fact of his resurrection. But now that Jesus' atoning death was completed, and he was alive in his resurrection body, there would be a transition in their relationship with him. Jesus was not saying to Mary that from now on they would relate less, but rather more. He'd promised the Holy Spirit (Jn. 14-16), who would soon indwell every one of his followers. Instead of being with them only when physically present, he would be in them and with them all the time. And they would continue to grow in intimacy with him in this transformed and transforming relationship.

Jesus told Mary Magdalene about this new way of relating to him because of his ascending to the Father. And then he gave her an assignment. Instead of her holding onto Jesus, she was now to take the Good News of Jesus to others. Mary was the first to be commissioned as a witness for the risen Lord Jesus. She was, first, a woman, and the testimony of a woman was not generally regarded as credible in that time and culture. Secondly, Mary was from Magdala, a notoriously wicked city. She had a reputation of having been possessed of seven demons prior to her being delivered by and following Jesus as her Lord (Lk. 8:2). She was not a likely poster girl for a new religious movement, in other words. But that seems to be the way God works. Paul says God intentionally chooses the weak, foolish, and lowly to demonstrate his grace and to show the power of the gospel doesn't reside in us but in God (1 Cor. 1:26-31; Eph. 1:19-20).

Robert W Dale (1829-95) was one of Great Britain's leading Congregational pastors and theologians who for much of his ministry failed to live and minister in the awareness and power of the Resurrection. He was brilliant, educated and polished, but lacking in power and fervor. One day as he was preparing an Easter sermon, "a realization of the risen Lord struck him with new power.

"'Christ is alive!' he said to himself. 'Alive—alive—alive!' He paused, and then said, 'Can that really be true? *Living* as really as I myself am?'

"He got up from his desk and began to walk about the study, repeating, 'Christ is living! Christ is living!'"

RW Dale "had known and believed this doctrine for years, but the reality of it overwhelmed him that day. From that time on, 'the living Christ' was the theme of his preaching, and he had his congregation sing an Easter hymn every Sunday morning. 'I want my people to get hold of the glorious fact that Christ is alive, and to rejoice over it; and Sunday, you know, is the day on which Christ left the dead'" (Wiersbe). The awareness of the risen Lord changes what preoccupies us and raises us to a new level of living and serving. Because Jesus lives, we also will live (Jn. 14:19). Death has lost its sting. The grave has been robbed of its victory (1 Cor. 15:54-58). The empty tomb is still before us as a place to meet the risen Lord.

Again, in the words of John Updike,

> *Let us not mock God with metaphor…*
> *let us walk through the door.*

He is risen!

# Doubting Thomas

## John 20:24-31

*[24] But Thomas (who was called the Twin), one of the twelve, was not with them when Jesus came. [25] So the other disciples told him, "We have seen the Lord." But he said to them, "Unless I see the mark of the nails in his hands and put my finger in the mark of the nails and my hand in his side, I will not believe."*

*[26] A week later his disciples were again in the house, and Thomas was with them. Although the doors were shut, Jesus came and stood among them and said, "Peace be with you." [27] Then he said to Thomas, "Put your finger here and see my hands. Reach out your hand and put it in my side. Do not doubt but believe." [28] Thomas answered him, "My Lord and my God!" [29] Jesus said to him, "Have you believed because you have seen me? Blessed are those who have not seen and yet have come to believe."*

*[30] Now Jesus did many other signs in the presence of his disciples, which are not written in this book. [31] But these are written so that you may come to believe that Jesus is the Messiah, the Son of God, and that through believing you may have life in his name.*

We're all familiar with the epithet, "Doubting Thomas." We use this term to describe anyone who has a skeptical bent, and it's almost always used in a derogatory way. *Webster's Dictionary* has the entry, "doubting Thomas," as "a habitually doubtful person." And, in fact, the first impression our text gives us of Thomas isn't a very favorable one. But as we consider the entire text, we'll gain perhaps a new appreciation for Thomas. More importantly, we can identify with him in our personal struggles with doubts and our growth toward a mature faith.

We pick on Thomas because he was alone in his doubt. On Resurrection Sunday the other disciples were privileged to see the Lord in his appearance to them, commissioning of them, and breathing the Holy Spirit into them. For whatever reason, Thomas wasn't there. Had almost any of the others not been there, they too might've been doubters until they'd seen Jesus for themselves.

Most who reflect on Thomas' character surmise that he was of a melancholy disposition. He was a pessimist, who tended to see the glass as "half empty instead of half full." And his pessimism may've contributed to his absence from the gathering of the disciples when Jesus appeared on that first Easter Sunday evening. He was alone, possibly sulking and brooding over his ominous future. Had he been there on that Resurrection night, he wouldn't have been "the doubter of the week." For whatever reasons, Thomas was at least a temporary doubter. His reaction to the testimony of the other disciples at first shows an almost modern proclivity to unbelief, but on closer inspection, his doubt was temporary, and we realize we've all been there.

Os Guinness wrote about the pilgrimage from doubt to faith in his book *In Two Minds: The Dilemma of Doubt and How to Resolve It*. He explains that the word "doubt" is from the Latin "dubitare," which means "two." To believe is to be in one mind. To disbelieve is to be in one mind also, the mind to reject a certain truth. To doubt is to waver between the two minds, and to be in a state of "doubleness," or "two-ness." Hopefully, this state of mind called doubt is a temporary one, and a stage of transition from unbelief to faith. I believe that doubt is a necessary experience in the pilgrimage of faith. As Guinness says, only God and certain madmen have no doubts.

Doubt is that experience of considering something, asking questions, and then moving beyond that doubt to new certainty. We don't get bogged down in doubt that hardens into militant unbelief, nor do we say we believe something without giving it serious consideration. There are many in the membership of the church today who've not given serious thought to the verity of the faith. They simply go along with the decision of others. Many have never thought through the truth claims of Christ and the Word, and thus cannot discern the error of false teachings.

The Christian faith requires that we believe what we cannot see with our eyes. Hebrews 11:1 says "Now faith is being sure of what we hope for and certain of what we do not see." But though we believe without seeing, we don't believe without considering (FF Bruce). Faith is not blind credulity and unthinking naiveté. I rather think Thomas had a desire to consider the truth of Jesus' resurrection.

Admittedly, some people have a greater inclination to doubt, just as some find it easier to believe. I was nurtured in the faith as a child, and my conversion came without a lot of struggle with doubt. My struggles came later, in high school and college, as I confronted ideas and issues that made me reexamine my faith. I was often in two minds and had to resolve doubts. But that was the way I grew in faith and understanding. Admittedly, I still have my moments of doubt when my faith is challenged by the mysteries of life and truth. In John's Gospel we see that Thomas was pessimistic by disposition, yet fiercely loyal (Jn. 11:16; 14:5). He tended to look on the dark side of things, and naturally struggled more with doubt than those of a more optimistic and cheerful disposition.

I remember a deacon in a church I served in a suburb of Cleveland, Ohio. This good man was from Tennessee, and had difficulty finding anything good about Cleveland, especially about its weather. He tended to see the dark side of just about anything. It was early spring, about this time of the year. We were finally beginning to pull out of a typically long, harsh and dreary winter. This Sunday morning, and I believe it was Easter Sunday, was unusually beautiful, sunny and warm. As I approached Cody in the hallway that morning, I thought, "What negative thing could he possibly say about this glorious day?" So, I said to him as cheerily as I could, "Good morning, Cody. It's a great day, isn't it?" "Yeah," he admitted begrudgingly. "But we'll pay for it tomorrow!" Poor fellow, he couldn't enjoy today for dreading tomorrow. But, thankfully, Cody Williams overcame his tendency to pessimism and doubt, and was a believer in the Lord Jesus, by the grace of God. I believe all true believers have spent some time in a state of doubt, and some more than others. But we shouldn't live there.

Doubt isn't the opposite of belief and faith. Doubt can work with faith, as we question the evidence and move on to greater faith. Unbelief, not doubt, is the opposite of faith/belief. Like the first disciples, including Thomas, we're to move beyond the state of questioning, considering and being in two minds about a matter.

The Chinese have a parable about doubt as the futile attempt to have one's feet in two boats. Sooner or later you must commit to one boat or the other, because eventually they will take you in different directions. To doubt is to delay, to hesitate between two opinions, and one who remains in doubt will eventually drown in the depths of unbelief.

How graciously the Lord accommodated himself to Thomas' doubt by making this special appearance the following Sunday night, in the same place and the same manner as he did the week before! Just as with the other disciples on Easter Sunday night, Jesus didn't come to them and say, "Shame on you!" He said to disciples who had forsaken and denied him, "Peace be with you." Jesus once again miraculously appeared in the locked room and spoke these gracious words. Jesus appeared this time specifically to meet Thomas' previously stated criterion for belief—that he put his hand into Jesus' scars in his hands and side, an offer Thomas found unnecessary. Seeing Jesus was enough for Thomas, who responded to Jesus with his worshipful confession of faith.

The disciples and Thomas had the unique experience of seeing Jesus in the flesh, and even of experiencing his full humanity, though now he was in his resurrection body. Jesus was resurrected with an immortal body, but it wasn't as a spirit that he was resurrected. His risen body was material, visible, tangible, and palpable. Yes, he could appear with a thought, and was no longer limited by time and space as he was during his 33 years of incarnation before the resurrection. Though different from his mortal body, his resurrection body was real, as real as our bodies.

Jesus said after Thomas' confession of faith that Thomas believed because he had seen but blessed are those who have not seen and yet have believed. He's referring to us. God brings us evidence of the gospel through the Word. It's not a word about something mystical but is the Word of God about his dealings in human history and about God's becoming a man in Jesus. It's a word about events that happened on this earth at a time in real history—Jesus' life, suffering, death, and resurrection. It's the Word calling us to confess and repent of sin and believe in Jesus and follow him as Lord. This Word that brings salvation is as real, close, and life-changing as the presence of the resurrection body of Jesus there in that Upper Room (Rom. 10: 14-17).

> *Peter writes in his first letter, "For you have been born again...through the living and enduring word of God"* (1 Pet. 1:23).

God brings the evidence we need for faith in Jesus. He gives us the evidence of the Word and the testimony of believers. This is a reminder to us who are believers that God uses us to lovingly and patiently bring with us those who are doubters and maybe even cynics. We shouldn't be fearful of or impatient with those who seem to be resistant to the truth, and who ask us hard and even offensive questions. Rather, we must be faithful in our witness, hopeful in our praying, and loving in our leading them to the place where they'll hear a saving word from God. The other disciples apparently didn't condemn Thomas, but quietly said to themselves, "You'll see for yourself and believe as we do."

Someone said that Thomas' problem was not so much his doubt as it was his absenteeism. In fact, Scripture tells us that faith doesn't come about apart from evidence, but rather through the preaching and hearing of the word of Christ (Rom. 10:17). Had he been with them on that first Easter Sunday night, he also would've believed. Faith is encouraged in the context of corporate worship, when we hear the word preached and sense the power of the presence of God (1 Cor. 14:24f). Faith is awakened in the minds and hearts of those willing to consider the evidence. Saving evidence comes through the Word and by the Holy Spirit, working through the reading, preaching and teaching of the Word, and confirmed in the testimony of believers. Those who absent themselves from worship, Bible reading, and the fellowship of God's people are growing weaker in faith.

In the words of a Greek scholar, Jesus literally said to Thomas, "Stop becoming unbelieving, and start becoming believing" (AT Robertson). In his pilgrimage of faith, Thomas had his admission of doubt, and moved on to his acceptance of the evidence for faith. The final stage of his experience was the assurance of faith. Thomas' faith sounds forth with joyous assurance.

We all know the skeptic's motto, "seeing is believing." That's what Thomas evidenced early on in our text. But when the Lord appeared to him, he responded with faith, and was thereby enabled to see/perceive something known only by faith, that is, the significance of the person of Jesus. Sense perception is not enough. When Thomas experienced the Lord Jesus, he was given grace to believe. He didn't even need to touch the wounds, a criterion he had earlier demanded. On the other hand, without grace to believe, it's possible to see overwhelming evidence and still not believe. But, for Thomas and for all people of faith, "believing is seeing." Thomas' seeing was met with God-given faith, which enabled him to make the great confession of faith.

Thomas' assurance of faith came by the confession of faith. Thomas was no longer the doubter as he exclaimed, "My *Lord* and my *God!*" What a statement of faith it was, directed toward the one who was crucified in total weakness and shame! Yet now he says Jesus is Lord over the religious and political empires that crucified him about ten days before. God-given faith alone allows us to believe that the Jesus who was crucified in weakness is now the risen, reigning Lord and God. Grace alone leads us to believe in and follow the Crucified, the one who saved us by his suffering and death, and who calls us to take this same path of weakness, suffering and death to self.

Thomas not only believed in the resurrection of Jesus, but now he believed in all his claims. It's not enough just to believe he arose, but that he lives as Lord and God. Thomas' assurance of faith came by the possession of faith. Thomas said with unequivocal conviction, "*My* Lord and *my* God!" Not only did Thomas possess Jesus. Jesus possessed Thomas. Tradition says that Thomas became an apostolic missionary, taking the gospel to India. He became one who believed in, loved and served Jesus as his Lord and Savior.

I've heard people reject the message of the gospel and the offer of eternal life, saying, "I'm just a doubting Thomas." Thomas doubted for only a week. Jesus says, "Stop doubting and believe." Thomas the Doubter became Thomas the Missionary, all because he admitted his doubt, accepted the evidence, and came into the subsequent assurance of faith. We need the possession of a personal faith in Jesus Christ. The faith to which John's Gospel calls us is not adherence to a creed, but "a dynamic believing in the person of Jesus" (Borchert).

We're either a doubting Thomas or we're a believing Thomas. We cannot keep our feet in two boats. Eventually two boats will shove off in different directions. We must honestly look at the evidence and believe.

# The Faith of a Young Girl
## Luke 1:26-45

*In the sixth month the angel Gabriel was sent by God to a town in Galilee called Nazareth, 27 to a virgin engaged to a man whose name was Joseph, of the house of David. The virgin's name was Mary. 28 And he came to her and said, "Greetings, favored one! The Lord is with you." 29 But she was much perplexed by his words and pondered what sort of greeting this might be. 30 The angel said to her, "Do not be afraid, Mary, for you have found favor with God. 31 And now, you will conceive in your womb and bear a son, and you will name him Jesus. 32 He will be great and will be called the Son of the Most High, and the Lord God will give to him the throne of his ancestor David. 33 He will reign over the house of Jacob forever, and of his kingdom there will be no end." 34 Mary said to the angel, "How can this be, since I am a virgin?" 35 The angel said to her, "The Holy Spirit will come upon you, and the power of the Most High will overshadow you; therefore the child to be born will be holy; he will be called Son of God. 36 And now, your relative Elizabeth in her old age has also conceived a son; and this is the sixth month for her who was said to be barren. 37 For nothing will be impossible with God." 38 Then Mary said, "Here am I, the servant of the Lord; let it be with me according to your word." Then the angel departed from her.*

Both Roman Catholics and Protestants have not treated Mary appropriately. We Protestants don't venerate her or pray to or through her, or even name our churches after her, but Mary is indeed worthy of our regard. The evidence of Scripture is that Mary was a godly young woman of moral purity when she was approached by the angel Gabriel. God in his foreknowledge chose Mary as a faithful steward of the overwhelming responsibility for the care and upbringing of Jesus, whom she understood to be the Messiah of God. For many years she struggled with her times of doubt about Jesus' unique role, but remained a faithful follower when Jesus began his public ministry. Mary wasn't perfect, but she was a disciple and Luke records in Acts 1:14 that Mary was with the other disciples in the Upper Room, waiting for the coming of the Holy Spirit on the Day of Pentecost. Because Mary was very human, and not divine, she's for us a fitting example of faith as an experience of growth.

God comes to the least suspecting because grace works in the hearts of those who have no claim upon him. God cannot give to those whose hands are already full of their own goodness and proud accomplishments. He comes to those prepared to receive him through their own sense of need and unworthiness. God brought this gracious appearance to Mary when she was totally unsuspecting and vulnerable to grace. And that's the way he may visit you as well. Mary wondered at this word of grace which was a surprising and awesome word. The undeserved yet desperately needed work of God in our behalf always appears great to us.

Gabriel told Mary that she was favored. Certainly, we wish to honor Mary as one of the great servants of the Lord, who played an important and unique role in salvation history. Yet the theme of our text is the greatness of God's grace. Mary was godly and devout, yet she was not chosen based on her merits, but simply by grace alone. Like you and me, she was undeserving and had done nothing nor could she do anything to earn God's favor. The angel went on to explain how the favor of God would give her the privilege of bearing the Holy Spirit-conceived Son of God.

Grace never comes to those of us who think we're deserving. It's always beyond our grasp or our power to earn. Our efforts at earning God's favor always come up short. As Mary continued to wonder, she asked, "How can this be, since I am a virgin?" She wasn't expressing unbelief, but rather wonder at the ways of God. Then the angel answered her question by saying that her miraculous, virgin conception would take place by the Holy Spirit. The angel reminded Mary that nothing is impossible with God. Faith that allows for God to rescue us is faith that focuses on his power and not on what we can do to save ourselves. I doubt if any come to saving faith without some sense of wonder and awe before the majesty of God. Perhaps this is part of what Jesus meant when he said that "anyone who will not receive the kingdom of God like a little child will never enter it" (Mark 10:15).

The power for deliverance and a new life is the same power that created the heavens and the earth; that conceived the Son of God within Mary; that accomplished our atonement with God through Christ's death on the cross; and that raised Christ Jesus from the dead on Easter morning (Eph. 1:19-20). The argument is one from greater to the lesser. If God's power has accomplished these things, how much more can we trust that his power will change our eternal destiny and even now, our very character? Nothing is impossible with God. God continues to strengthen our faith and even accommodates us during times of weakness. His grace sustains and encourages us as with Mary.

Throughout her spiritual pilgrimage, Mary experienced the adequacy of God's grace. Her life would not be easy. When Mary and Joseph took the baby Jesus to the temple for his circumcision and ritual purification, they were met by the devout Simeon and Anna, aged prophets who recognized the baby Jesus as the fulfillment of their messianic hopes. Simeon prophesied to Mary that "a sword will pierce your own soul too" (Luke 2:35). Perhaps Mary remembered this prophecy as she stood at the foot of the cross, as her Son was crucified for her and for all the sins of the world (John 19:25-27). Throughout her life Mary no doubt wondered at the awesome grace, power and adequacy of God in her life.

I think of the Christmas song by John Jacob Niles:

> *I wonder as I wander out under the sky,*
> *That Jesus the Savior should come for to die,*
> *For poor ornery sinners like you and like I.*
> *I wonder as I wander out under the sky.*

*Here am I, the servant of the Lord; let it be with me according to your word,"* was her response. For Mary to become the mother of Jesus, for her to experience within her womb the miracle of the virgin conception, she had to submit to the work of grace, first through trusting. It's probably impossible for us to fully appreciate what a miracle of grace it was for this young girl Mary to trust in this word from the angel. We have millennia of church history and theology to fall back upon, but this announcement from the angel would have been contrary to all previous human experience and reason. For her to receive this miracle, she needed to trust the word of God, which is faith.

Of herself, Mary would not have the faith to trust the word of God. No doubt Mary was of a humble yet devout upbringing and was acquainted with the Scriptures that promised the Messiah, who would deliver his people from their sins. Yet the word of God is more than just a dead letter but accompanied by the Spirit of God becomes alive. The Holy Spirit touched her heart as one who was chosen in Christ "before the creation of the world" (Ephesians 1:4). She had not sought God. He sought her and drew her to himself and gave Mary grace to believe. Only grace could have enabled Mary to believe in the miracle of the virgin conception of the Son of God. To me, even physical birth is a miracle.

Mary had grace to believe that the eternal Son of the Most High would be conceived miraculously, and be born as a helpless infant, in primitive and crude conditions. The Son of God, the Savior of the world, would in his incarnation need the care, protection and provisions of his peasant parents!

The Son of God was to be conceived within Mary's womb by the overshadowing power of the Holy Spirit (Luke 1:35). She had nothing to do with Jesus' conception, except to be the vessel in which the Holy Spirit would work.

John seems to have this miracle of conversion in mind when he writes in his prologue to the gospel that, "To all who received him, to those who believed in his name, he gave the right to become children of God—children born not of natural descent, nor of human decision or a husband's will, but born of God" (John 1:12-13).

We aren't Christians because of our heritage or any natural goodness or ability. Nor are we excluded from faith and from inclusion in God's family because of our lack of spiritual or religious pedigree. If that had been God's way, he would have chosen the betrothed wife of a high priest and/or ruler of the Sanhedrin. But instead, God simply chose a young girl bereft of credentials. Apart from faith, church rituals and routines mean nothing to God, who knows the heart and is seeking those who will be open to a personal, life-changing relationship and a life of discipleship.

Mary was willing to believe, trust and obey the word of the Lord (Luke 1:38, 45). She trusted everything she knew about God with everything she had to offer him. Her faith would grow and mature the more she pondered in her heart (Luke 2:19). But God had already begun to do his good work in her, which he would bring to completion (Philippians 1:6). Her submitting to God's work of grace involved also her obeying. Young Mary's response was one of complete obedience: *"Here am I, the servant of the Lord; let it be with me according to your word."*

And obeying for Mary would involve growing in grace, a life of continual trust and obedience and growing in the grace and knowledge of the Lord Jesus Christ (2 Peter 3:18). At the time of the angel's announcement to her, Mary had no way of knowing how costly grace would be in her life. She would need to grow in grace to face the challenges that lay ahead for her. She would face misunderstandings and unbelief of her conception and pregnancy as a virgin, by her pledged husband to be and by all the people who knew her. Apart from God's intervention and protection (as when the angel explained Mary's condition to Joseph, Matthew 1:18-25), Mary's life would have been in danger and certainly ruined.

As one commentator wrote, "A young unmarried girl who became pregnant risked disaster." Unless the father of the child agreed to marry her, she would probably remain unmarried for life. If her own father rejected her, she could be forced into begging or prostitution in order to earn her living. And Mary, with her story about being made pregnant by the Holy Spirit, risked being considered crazy as well. Still Mary said, despite the possible risks, "Let it be with me according to your word." Being the mother of the Messiah would not be an easy road for Mary. And the life of grace and obedience doesn't mean our lives will be easy.

The miracle of faith changes your life immediately, but also takes place over time. As a diamond is forged through centuries of intense pressure, so is the character of Christlikeness forged through times and years of struggle of soul and spiritual warfare. Most children are assessed by how much they resemble their parents. But, because of the Holy Spirit who would fill Mary's life, she would become like the Son whom she carried within her womb. Jesus, in his physical appearance, may have shared some of Mary's physical traits. But in his character, he was perfectly like his heavenly Father.

Of all my siblings, I bore the most resemblance to my father, the late Ray Roberts. When I was much younger, there were places in Ohio and North Carolina where often those of my father's generation would say, "You must be Ray's boy!" Would that I were compared wherever I go with my Lord Jesus and my heavenly Father!

This is the ongoing miracle of faith, Mary's faith, believing the impossible that happened *for* us and that takes place *within* us. Just as Mary's faith was a miracle, so is our conversion. Only a work of grace can move our hearts to believe and forge in us over the years of time the character of Christlikeness. If the Holy Spirit has begun a work in you, you're experiencing the same power that shaped the universe and that raised Jesus from the grave. I pray that you'll not allow this Christmas Season to slip away without experiencing the miracle of faith that brings a changed life and destiny.

# Discipleship Is Following Jesus

## Luke 9:57-62

> *⁵⁷ As they were going along the road, someone said to him, "I will follow you wherever you go." ⁵⁸ And Jesus said to him, "Foxes have holes, and birds of the air have nests; but the Son of Man has nowhere to lay his head." ⁵⁹ To another he said, "Follow me." But he said, "Lord, first let me go and bury my father." ⁶⁰ But Jesus said to him, "Let the dead bury their own dead; but as for you, go and proclaim the kingdom of God." ⁶¹ Another said, "I will follow you, Lord; but let me first say farewell to those at my home." ⁶² Jesus said to him, "No one who puts a hand to the plow and looks back is fit for the kingdom of God."*

The key word in our text is, "follow" (vv. 57, 59, 61). Two of the three would-be disciples declare their intentions of following Jesus and the other is directly challenged by Jesus to follow him. A disciple is one who learns by following the master-teacher and those of us who claim the name "Christian" are necessarily followers of Christ. This passage of Scripture for today has been called a travel narrative, which begins with the phrase, "As they were walking along...." Jesus was on the move and we might say that the crucified, risen Lord Jesus is still on the move and we must learn what it means to travel with him, i.e., to follow him.

Dietrich Bonhoeffer (1906-1945) was a brilliant theologian and pastor whose preaching, leadership and writings challenged the complacency of Christians who treated saving grace as something cheap and undemanding. Young Bonhoeffer himself declined the way of safety and because of his opposition to the Nazi regime was executed in Flossenberg at the age of 39. When Bonhoeffer was only 30, his most influential book, *The Cost of Discipleship*, was published. In this exposition of the teachings of Jesus that speak about discipleship, Bonhoeffer makes a clear and convincing case that discipleship is not optional if one makes a claim to have received saving grace and the gift of eternal life. Bonhoeffer lived up to his own definition of the Christian life as one of discipleship, himself following Jesus to a martyr's death.

In my tradition, the concept of salvation is almost exclusively bound up with simply accepting what Jesus has done for us on the cross. Everlasting heaven or hell are presented as the options facing the sinner, who then is asked to decide between these two alternatives—a real "no-brainer." In presenting the offer of salvation, the evangelist simply tells what Jesus has done and asks only that the would-be convert believe the fact of the gospel and ask Jesus to forgive one's sins (if the subject of sin is broached at all) and come into the forgiven sinner's heart. Then the new "convert" is assured of the gift of eternal life and is told to never doubt this guaranteed salvation. This so-called free grace, however is, in the words of Bonhoeffer, "cheap grace," and is not the kind of grace that works through faith as a commitment to Jesus as Lord.

As Jesus and his disciples were traveling on the road, someone came up to Jesus and volunteered. *The Message* paraphrases verse 57 as saying, "On the road someone asked if he could go along. 'I'll go with you, wherever,' he said." Reading this one can almost sense the flippancy of this statement. Certainly, Jesus knew the superficiality of this volunteer. Here was a would-be disciple who obviously was unwilling to pay the price of following Jesus. His "volunteerism" seemed based solely upon the attraction of Jesus.

The Gospels are filled with pictures of how individuals and even multitudes were attracted to Jesus. He was, after all, a great miracle worker and teacher. His teachings revealed great insight into the word of God and human nature. Jesus' miracles provided healing for the sick, sight for the blind, hearing for the deaf and wholeness for the lame. The Lord Jesus did exorcisms of demons, feeding the hungry multitudes and even resurrection from death. And there was something attractive about the very character and persona of Jesus. The worst of sinners, those who were regarded as outcasts by the religious insiders, were drawn to Jesus because of his unconditional love and acceptance. So, this volunteer came as did many others, seeking to join up with Jesus for what Jesus could do for him.

Cheap grace is being offered wholesale these days. In this age and culture of the voracious consumer, the North American church is offering a gospel of accommodation to the needs and tastes of the consumer, the would-be disciple. Consumers are being drawn to the Jesus who meets every felt need and enables us to reach our preferred goals. Thousands, perhaps millions of people are drawn into the church each year and even profess faith in the Jesus who "will do for them," making their lives bearable or even more successful and prosperous. Sadly, many of these people will never be confronted with the superficiality of this ersatz version of "faith," and will never know the joy or the converting power of the true gospel of the kingdom, the life of discipleship. Tragically they will be deceived into thinking that the version of "grace" offered them is the real thing.

Jesus spoke about and faced increasing rejection, opposition and hostility, which would eventually be consummated in his arrest, trial and crucifixion (9:22, 44; 17:25; 20:17). Jesus warns one would-be follower about his dependence on the hospitality of others to give him shelter. *The Message* again brings our text to life in a present-day setting: "Jesus was curt: 'Are you ready to rough it? We're not staying in the best inns, you know'."

As we decide about answering the call to follow Jesus in a life of discipleship we must answer for ourselves whether it's worth it. G Campbell Morgan (1863-1945) said that when Jesus spoke of not having his own home he did so, not remorsefully with self-pity, but with joy and jubilation. "When next you quote these words of Jesus," said the great English preacher, "don't pity him. He does not need your pity. Pity yourself rather if you have a home that holds you back, when Christ wants you out upon the high places of the world….Pity yourself if you are rooted anywhere, when he would have you move to some other place in your pilgrimage with him towards the cross and for human redemption." Our greatest compensation in discipleship is to know and enjoy Jesus himself, his fellowship and purpose for our lives, as we join him on pilgrimage.

As Jesus continued his way, he saw another would-be disciple and said to him, "Follow me "(60). In this case, it appears that this man has a problem with priorities in his life. Like the first man, he seems to have an interest in following Jesus, but something stands in his way. This second would-be follower seemed to have a legitimate and even a biblical right to hesitate in following Jesus. He asks permission to first go and bury his father. Every conscientious Jewish son recognized his responsibility to take care of his father's burial. This was "a religious duty having precedence over all else." In fact, this was a common fear among Jews who had no male son, that there would be no one to see to his proper funeral and burial. This would-be disciple must have thought that Jesus would honor his rationale for postponing obedience. One can even use verses from the Bible to rationalize disobedience to Christ. Surely Jesus would not argue with Scripture! But Jesus knows when we're seeking to justify disobedience even based on our use of Scripture when it suits our purpose. I've known of parents who discouraged their young adult children from following Jesus to the mission field by quoting to them verses like the ones that speak about honoring father and mother.

It would be unlikely that Jesus would hinder the fulfillment of genuine family responsibilities. He seemed to perceive an unwillingness to give priority to following him. For one who has not given Jesus absolute priority, there will always be a series of things and events and excuses that will keep one from following him. Whatever the case, Jesus told him to let the dead bury their own dead. What he referred to was the fact that there were plenty of spiritually dead people who were available to take care of these duties, which would be overseen by responsible family members. Jesus was not opposed to carrying out family responsibilities but rather was upholding the priority that must be given to him above all other relationships and commitments. The choice we face is in making Jesus the Lord of our lives. When he is Lord, then all other relationships become secondary to us (e.g. Lk. 14:25-27).

Genuine faith that responds to the grace of God in Christ is life-changing and priority rearranging. If one still has the same loyalties and basically the same lifestyle after that "profession of faith" then there is no evidence of a possession of faith. If worship is no different and has no priority for you, then you haven't made the discipleship choice. If your spending habits are the same and there is no priority in your giving to the kingdom of God and no change in the priority of your time investments, then you haven't made the discipleship choice of following Jesus. Faith that saves is faith that works in obedience.

The choices that we make are not always between the overtly good and bad things of life. To follow Jesus means that he must take precedence over even the good things he has given to us, including even our families. It's not unusual to make an idol of one's family, and in the name of being godly, Christian parents we can place our children above the place that God should have in our homes. And, because Jesus promises the blessing of "these other things" being added to us (Matt. 6:33), he'll see to it that our children's needs are met. I've seen children's lives wrecked by well-intentioned and overly strict or overly indulgent parents who placed on their children the priority that God alone deserves. And children whose parents give priority to God and whose lives are centered in Christ are privileged to receive the blessings of God.

Jesus knew the hearts of these would-be disciples and one element missing in all three was a passion for Jesus and his kingdom, a passion that would be necessary to sustain their perseverance in following him. Like the others, this man was sincerely drawn to Jesus and something in him wanted to follow, to give his life to Jesus. But also, there was a reluctance to give all to him. Bonhoeffer says that this man, when he came to Jesus, already had his career mapped out. He simply wanted Jesus to bless his plans. For this man, there was not a heart to fully obey. For him and for us, to delay is to disobey. He wanted to follow Jesus as a matter of convenience and expected Jesus to wait on his agenda and allow him to first fulfill his personal plans. But Jesus, remember, is traveling, on the move. And if we delay, he moves on without us.

No one can follow Jesus while looking back, says Jesus. He will be as useless as a farmer trying to plow while looking backwards. He can make a mess of things (62). Looking back takes us off course, just as a farmer begins to plow crooked furrows. Such backward looking and being distracted makes us useless in kingdom of God service. And we can make a mess of our lives.

A focused will and passionate heart for Jesus is what Paul expressed when he wrote,

> "Not that I have already obtained all this, or have already been made perfect, but I press on to take hold of that for which Christ Jesus took hold of me. Brothers, I do not consider myself yet to have taken hold of it. But one thing I do: Forgetting what is behind and straining towards what is ahead, I press on towards the goal to win the prize for which God has called me heavenwards in Christ Jesus" (Phil.1:21; 3:10-14).

Paul knew there's no substitute for union with Christ, who invites us to join him, not in a life of drudgery, but one of joy and the enjoyment of being with Christ.

My father, who was my childhood hero, liked to tell about the time he let me help him paint the back porch of our home. My contribution was minimal, and maybe even detrimental to the project, but he let me swipe away, and he would touch up my misapplied strokes. Several times during the project, I would break the silence to ask him, "Daddy, are we painting?" He would assure me several times with words I loved to hear, when I would ask again, emphasizing the word, "we:" "Daddy, are *we* painting?" "Yes, son, we are painting." Following Jesus brings the joy of assurance that we are walking and serving with him.

Only when we have this kind of passion for Jesus do we know we'll follow him with faithfulness, undivided loyalty and perseverance. Only with this passion would we remain faithful through life's trials and disappointments and during the "dry" periods when prayers seem unanswered and our emotions are largely negative. This passion for Jesus is what enables those who're being persecuted and are even facing martyrdom to remain faithful in their witness and stand for Jesus. In my latter years, I continue to face the possibility of paying a price to follow Jesus, one that will test my faith, obedience and willingness to sacrifice things held dear. It may mean the testing of our moral convictions.

To follow Jesus is to join him in his work of loving our neighbor, caring for the needy and oppressed, standing for the cause of justice and mercy, expressing concern and practicing forgiveness, joining Jesus wherever he goes. He calls us to himself. And if we would be his disciples we'll come after him, abide in him and follow him wherever he may lead us. He's always on the move

# An Advent Witness
## John 1:1-9

> *1 In the beginning was the Word, and the Word was with God, and the Word was God. ² He was in the beginning with God. ³ All things came into being through him, and without him not one thing came into being. What has come into being ⁴ in him was life, and the life was the light of all people. ⁵ The light shines in the darkness, and the darkness did not overcome it.*
>
> *⁶ There was a man sent from God, whose name was John. ⁷ He came as a witness to testify to the light, so that all might believe through him. ⁸ He himself was not the light, but he came to testify to the light. ⁹ The true light, which enlightens everyone, was coming into the world.* This is the word of the Lord.

Perhaps as at no other time of the year, Advent is an exceptionally advantageous time to witness to family, friends and associates as we share the meaning of the Christmas celebration.

Years ago, while serving a church in Wichita, Kansas, a public school elementary music teacher in our church read a little book about the historical events of Christmas (an approach to "the Bible as history") to her public school elementary music classes. She was summarily informed by one of her second graders, whose parents might have belonged to the American Civil Liberties Union, or the Freedom from Religion Foundation, that she wasn't supposed to talk about Jesus in school. She replied that she was telling them that the history of Christmas is centered in the birth of Jesus. When she taught about other national holidays, like Thanksgiving, she told about Governor Bradford, so when she taught about Christmas she told about Jesus. She taught about Jesus at Christmas just as she taught about the presidents on Presidents Day. In other words, Christmas is meaningless apart from at least the mention of Jesus. As followers of Christ, it's appropriate to talk about him at Christmas.

John the Evangelist tells us about the role of John the Baptist as a witness to Christ. The word and concept used in the Gospel of John for witness runs throughout the book. "Witness" is used 14 times in the noun form and 33 times as a verb. Our text tells us this forerunner of Jesus, the last of the Old Testament prophets, was a bridge between the Old and the New Covenant (Testaments). John the Baptist/Baptizer was a man whose diet consisted of locusts and wild honey and who preached a message of judgment and the call to repentance in the desert wilderness. His unusual, counter-cultural lifestyle is an indication he may have belonged to the prophetic Qumran community.

Regardless of any eccentricities, John the Baptist models for us the life and ministry of an authentic witness in contrast to the many false witnesses of his day. Instead of being called John the Baptizer, a more accurate moniker would be John the Witness.

An authentic witness is a mortal human being, created by God in his image. John the Baptist was a unique personality for certain! And God has created you and me in our distinctiveness for his pleasure and glory. Never despise what God has created, and trust that he is continuing to complete his creation in you as he shapes your character into his likeness. God has created us to reflect his glory.

John the Baptist was one who was sent from God, which means he had a personal relationship with God. He could point others to God because he himself knew him and not just about him.

I know a man who's retired from ministry, living in North Kansas City, Missouri. His job now is with a travel agency, and he specializes in travel to Australia. I asked Wendell about Australia, since this is a place I've never visited. He confessed he hasn't been there either. He's in somewhat of a professional dilemma. Evidently, he must sell several trips to Australia before he can earn his own trip to the Land Down Under. I would think he's at a distinct disadvantage of having to sell folks on a place he has never been himself (I wonder till this day if he's ever made his first trip to Australia!).

Of course, an authentic witness to Jesus Christ is someone who knows Jesus personally, and is sent from him to tell others about that relationship. How can you lead someone else to go where you haven't been yourself? An authentic witness is one who can relate a fresh experience with God. Inquirers want to know the difference a relationship with Jesus makes in your life today. They want to know what he has done for you lately.

Jesus told his enemies about the greatness of John the Baptist, and how they refused to repent at his powerful preaching. He said, "I tell you, among those born of women there is no one greater than John;" Jesus added some amazing words that should humble each one of us: "Yet the one who is least in the kingdom of God is greater than he" (Lk. 7:28). John the Baptist was Jesus' forerunner and the link between the Old and the New Covenants. We're privileged to belong to the New Covenant and to live this side of the resurrection of Jesus. We're also this side of Pentecost and are indwelt by the Holy Spirit. We're able to live our entire lives in the full measure of the Holy Spirit and are part of the eternal Kingdom through the church of the risen Lord.

We should live as authentic witnesses, daily led by the Holy Spirit. We belong to the powers of the New Age of the living Christ. Every morning when you step outside your house, you should live as one sent from God, with the incredible privilege of representing him and giving a witness for him. Through Jesus-shaped lives of love, and obedience, and by our words about Jesus, God will work through us even in ways beyond the work of John the Baptist. We're allowed to introduce people to the power of the completed work of Jesus. We join God in his work of drawing people to himself. God wants to empower us that we might become his witnesses he's selected and is sending as missional people in the power of the Holy Spirit.

As one has said, these words describing the appointment of John the Baptist as "sent from God" are "exalted terms," which are used of Jesus in (16:27) and of the Holy Spirit (15:26). You and I too are chosen and called to this exalted position as a witness and an ambassador for Christ (2 Cor. 5:20).

One book I recall reading in high school was *The Ugly American*, about American diplomats and other US officials in Southeast Asia, whose self-indulgent and culturally insensitive lifestyle and character brought disgrace to our country at a critical time in our relationship with Southeast Asia. And there have been and are plenty of "ugly ambassadors for Christ," who bring discredit and make a negative image before the watching world.

You and I are created, chosen and sent on a high mission as ambassadors for Christ (2 Cor. 5:20) that no one else can fill. We must approach our task as witnesses with humble dependence on God's power to enable us to be his best representatives to those to whom God is sending us in our unique spheres of influence, with family, friends, colleagues and fellow students.

Our text is clear that John the Baptist was subordinate to Jesus, the true Light (8). This attitude of humility is seen particularly where John states his subordinate relationship to Jesus:

"He must become greater; I must become less" (Jn. 3:30).

Jesus himself, speaking about John the Baptist, said, "John was a lamp that burned and gave light, and you chose for a time to enjoy his light" (Jn. 5:35). Jesus said John had a role to point others to him who is the true Light.

As the Apostle Paul said, we too, unlike the "superstars" who denigrated Paul and his leadership, are to say that Christ is our life, and to live is Christ (Phil. 1:21). Jesus is the Light of the world, and we're called to be lights in the world (Matt. 5:14), but like John the Baptist, our light is derived from and dependent on the true Light of the World (Jn. 8:12).

Our world doesn't want to see people who have all the answers in themselves. Our world needs to see ordinary, struggling people who're learning to trust a great God. Your world around you need to see in your life an authentically dependent person who is learning to trust an almighty, loving, and faithful God. They need to see that you, like John the Baptist, are under the Lordship of Christ.

I'm seeking to be a faithful witness to those in my traffic patterns of ordinary, daily life. If I'm not having a particularly wonderful day, when someone asks me "how're ya doin'? should I say the word that's become a cliché, "perfect"? Maybe they need to hear an honest word, to know I share the coming struggles and ups and downs of life. I need to be real with them, but also relate that God is my strength.

Although not above common struggles and failures, an authentic witness is one who has a sense of responsibility for others, and realizes this is a personal, irreplaceable task. It's lifelong and non-negotiable. Our text says that John the Baptist "came as a witness…." And we know he died violently as a martyr after his faithful ministry was completed (Matt. 14:1-12).

The word in our text for witness is "martureo." From that word we get the English word, "martyr," which means one who dies for his/her faith. The early witnesses were so faithful to Christ they were willing to die for their faith, and often did. Thus, the word for witness became synonymous with one who dies for her or his faith, as would John the Baptist, who was an authentic witness.

God has called every one of us to be a missional Christian, which is one who is on mission to take Christ out into the world, instead of trying to bring the lost into the church or simply sending others to the mission field. Our focus is not just to disseminate information about Christ, but to do whatever it takes, in the power, wisdom and love of the Spirit, to lead them to faith in Christ.

Being a faithful witness, as John the Baptist knew, requires the grace of God and the anointing of the Spirit in our lives. Your witness requires the divine power of God to sustain you and to encourage you, especially when it seems your witness is spurned and ineffective. Your part is to be faithful. John the Baptist was faithful to fulfill his calling. Even though his life ending in a violent martyrdom, he had finished the work that God had appointed him to do. And this is all that the Lord requires of you—to be faithful, whether your witness appears to be immediately successful.

In this Gospel of John, we have a summary of the effectiveness and fruitfulness of John the Baptist's witness. He had prepared the way for the Lord through preparing the hearts of many people to come to Jesus (10:40-42). Like John the Baptist, you may not live to see all the fruit of your life, but in eternity you'll realize that God honored your faithful witness to family, friends and those you have perhaps long forgotten.

A witness must take a stand and cannot remain neutral. The language John the Evangelist uses for John the Baptist is "courtroom language." If you take your stand in the witness box and testify that such-and-such is the truth of the matter, you're no longer neutral. You've committed yourself. Just as a witness in a courtroom cannot remain silent, and that the life of the defendant might depend on us, so we must be faithful, bold witnesses for Christ in behalf of those under condemnation.

Let's ask the Lord God to make us aware of unique opportunities to share Christ this Advent Season, perhaps by inviting guests to our home and seeing symbolic Christmas decorations and hearing from us the message of Christ's birth. It's perfectly legal in this country to talk about Jesus in your home! And we have better news than you read about in the papers or hear in the countless ads on television.

Effective witnessing is done through one-on-one relationships. And in our increasingly secular culture (including increasingly secular holidays!), relationships are perhaps the only way of reaching the unconverted and unchurched, who aren't likely to visit our worship services.

Brian Harbour tells about Palmer Ofuoku, although not a Christian, was placed in a mission school in Nigeria because his parents knew he would receive a good education there. He attended the school for years yet remained an adherent of a traditional African religion. One year a new missionary came to the school who began to develop close relationships with the students, including Palmer, and eventually led this young Nigerian to Christ. Palmer Ofuoku explained the missionary's influence, saying "He built a bridge of friendship to me, and Jesus walked across."

We are God's Advent witnesses, called to build bridges of friendship to those we know and are yet to meet. As we do so, Jesus will walk across.

# We Are People of the Cross

## 1 Corinthians 1:18-31

> [18] *For the message about the cross is foolishness to those who are perishing, but to us who are being saved it is the power of God.* [19] *For it is written,*
>
> > *"I will destroy the wisdom of the wise,*
> > *and the discernment of the discerning I will thwart."*
>
> [20] *Where is the one who is wise? Where is the scribe? Where is the debater of this age? Has not God made foolish the wisdom of the world?* [21] *For since, in the wisdom of God, the world did not know God through wisdom, God decided, through the foolishness of our proclamation, to save those who believe.* [22] *For Jews demand signs and Greeks desire wisdom,* [23] *but we proclaim Christ crucified, a stumbling block to Jews and foolishness to Gentiles,* [24] *but to those who are the called, both Jews and Greeks, Christ the power of God and the wisdom of God.* [25] *For God's foolishness is wiser than human wisdom, and God's weakness is stronger than human strength.*
>
> [26] *Consider your own call, brothers and sisters: not many of you were wise by human standards, not many were powerful, not many were of noble birth.* [27] *But God chose what is foolish in the world to shame the wise; God chose what is weak in the world to shame the strong;* [28] *God chose what is low and despised in the world, things that are not, to reduce to nothing things that are,* [29] *so that no one might boast in the presence of God.* [30] *He is the source of your life in Christ Jesus, who became for us wisdom from God, and righteousness and sanctification and redemption,* [31] *in order that, as it is written, "Let the one who boasts, boast in the Lord."*

Some things don't ever change! The church in first century Corinth met with problems like those faced today. In retrospect, the culture and mindset of ancient Corinth presaged that of western society today. It was a culture that worshiped its heroes, who promoted style over substance. Their heroes were the orators and scholars that articulated the conventional wisdom of the day. Those who could make the best appearance and impression were the ones who became the leaders, whether their speech and conduct had integrity or not.

The Greek religious mentality was able to divorce, in good New Age fashion, spirituality from revealed truth, and conventionally accepted behavior from ethics and morals. A person could be considered spiritually elite and his or her teaching regarded as philosophically profound, even if their ethics and morals were promiscuous. Even some in the congregation of the church in Corinth were caught up in the spirit of the age and fancied themselves as being people of a specially-endowed wisdom. They worshiped their oratorical heroes like today's westerners do our super athletes, musicians and movie stars. The Corinthians were enamored by their public speaking celebrities who seemed to have the most power and control over their audience. As is often true today, people valued style over substance. Paul reminds these misled congregants that they had forgotten the message of the gospel, which is centered in the cross of Jesus. The message of the cross is the source and essence of real wisdom and is the only power that can eternally and profoundly change a human life.

The disciple of Christ is one who is committed to the message of the cross of Jesus as the reference point for the wisdom that the world so desperately needs. Whereas the world's wisdom begins and ends with futility, the cross of Jesus Christ reveals the truth about a holy and loving God. The cross shows that Jesus, the crucified now risen Lord, is the truth of God. To know and follow him is to come to grips with our sin, and to be in possession of a life-changing relationship with a loving God. But to the fallen world, whether in first century Corinth, or in Madison, Wisconsin, the message of the cross is foolishness. Peterson's *Message* paraphrases verse 18...

> *"The Message that points to Christ on the Cross seems like sheer silliness to those hell-bent on destruction..."*

The Jews of the first century regarded the message of the cross as a stumbling block (23). The message is that all religious effort to merit salvation by works is futile. Only by the undeserved gift of the cross-can sinners be made right with holy God. So, the religious dismiss the cross as an offensive replacement for their religious efforts and a nullification of all their acquired merit. It's scandalous to the dutifully religious to think that pagan outsiders will get the same treatment and eternal reward as they.

The Geeks, the secular folks, regarded Paul's message of the cross as sheer silliness. How could a crucified Jew claim to be a savior? The philosophy of Paul's world centered on what specially-endowed and privileged Greeks could know and articulate with eloquence. The culturally elite dismissed Paul and his preaching about the cross as "sheer silliness." But Paul knew that the message of the cross was God's revelation of true wisdom, and those who believe this message are given the true wisdom of God.

The child of God is one whose life has been changed by the cross of Christ. Our being in a love relationship with God is because of his sheer mercy and grace extended from the cross on which Christ Jesus suffered and died for our sins. The cross is the greatest fact about our lives and the center of our witness and our message as followers of Christ. And we can expect our world to regard the message of the cross as foolishness in the dim light of our information-glutted yet unwise age. We know that apart from Christ's atoning suffering and death on the cross we too would be without hope and without God in this world (Ephesians 2:12).

Robert Webber describes "Wal-Mart churches" that provide what people want, and not necessarily what they need. The Millennial Generation, those born since 1980, are looking for something authentic in place of ersatz Christianity. They're looking back to traditions like the early church and the Reformation to find examples of believers who held to, lived by, and proclaimed the true gospel of the cross.

The Holy Scriptures, containing the gospel of the cross, can make us "wise for salvation through faith in Christ Jesus" (2 Timothy 3:15, NIV). The cross is the only way of salvation. If there could have been any other way, then the cup would have passed from the Savior. The way of the cross is the wisdom of God, telling us about our sin, and about a holy God who must punish sin. For the born-again, there's an entrance into the life in the Spirit. For those to whom God gives grace to believe, there's also given an understanding of his word and will.

I've known truly wise people who lacked formal education, yet who knew the Lord Jesus and the Bible. Though deficient in cultural sophistication, they were educated in the truth about God and themselves. They understand life and God's creation and purposes far more than even the most scholarly who don't know the wisdom of God. The foolishness of God is wiser than man's wisdom.

The Apostle Paul understood the cross to be the *summum bonum* of his life and ministry, the supreme good in his life from which all other blessings were derived. Apart from the message and power of the cross Paul knew he would be eternally separated from God. That's why he was devoted to proclaiming the message of the cross and to live by its power, and even boast in the cross as how God used to change his life forever (Galatians 6:14).

By God's gracious initiative, when the message of the cross is preached, he sends forth his convicting Spirit into the hearts of his chosen. Therefore, Paul determined to know nothing but the cross when he preached. He made the cross the central theme of his preaching. His resolve in Corinth was his resolve everywhere, and that was to make the message of the cross central. Our interpretation of all of Scripture must be against the backdrop of the cross.

The great 19th Century British preacher, CH Spurgeon, in one of his lectures to his students at his pastor's college, admonished them in all their sermons, whatever the text and theme, to "make a beeline to the cross."

The recent passing away of Billy Graham brought to my memory a turning point in the world-famous evangelist's life. Young Graham was being influenced by Charles Templeton, who was enamored by liberal theology, and wanted his friend Billy to take a broad view of Scripture and not "limit" himself to a narrow preaching of the simple gospel message.

Billy went for a prayer walk in the California woods where he was leading a Bible conference and confessed to God there were things in the Bible that he could not explain, yet he was going to, from that moment on, preach with authority the simple gospel. Said young Graham: "So I went back and got my Bible, and I went out in the moonlight. And I got to a stump and put the Bible on the stump, and I knelt, and said, 'Oh, God; I cannot prove certain things. I cannot answer some of the questions Chuck is raising and some of the people are raising, but I accept this Book by faith as the Word of God.'"

Thousands can be grateful that Billy Graham made this resolve, which reflected Paul's. We need to go deep in our understanding of the Word, and we must appreciate serious biblical scholarship, yet there's much in Scripture we'll not understand till eternity. Whatever other themes we address, our perspective must ever be shaped by the Cross, with confidence in the power of the simple message of Christ crucified.

Paul says we have no reason to feel proud or to boast about our spiritual knowledge or giftedness. In the Greco-Roman world pride and boasting were considered virtues, and humility was a sign of weakness, a "dog virtue". Yet Paul reminds the church we belong to a new community of the redeemed who all know we're debtors to the grace of God and find our strength in dependence on him.

Jesus announced he had come to give the gospel and deliverance to the poor, who were so neglected and often omitted from the realm of the temple. So, the social composition of the church should be a sign of God's choice of the foolish, the weak, the low, and despised. As one said, "We should look around our congregations on Sunday. If we see too many of the educated, the powerful, and the wealthy and too few of the poor, we should ask ourselves whether we have somehow gone astray from God's purpose, distorted the gospel of the cross, and fallen into captivity to human wisdom. Paul does not exactly condemn education, power, and wealth in this passage, but merely suggests that God has made it foolish and irrelevant" with those he's chosen (Hayes).

God shows himself strong in our weak, cruciform lives. He delights in using those of us who're ordinary, and can't point to self, and say "look what I did for God, with all my wealth, wisdom, learning and influence." Ordinary folks like us are to take the message of the cross to those in need, who recognize their need. The poor and broken are the quickest to do so. The Apostle to the Gentiles understood well that the way to the hearts of the religious Jews and the pagan Greeks was not by human wisdom, but by lives characterized by the cross and being remade into Christ's likeness.

As followers of Jesus, the cross is to be central in our lives. Our rootless world is yearning for the healing grace of God, and we've the answer, not in theology, but in the person of Christ Jesus. We share, not out of our power, wealth, and worldly influence, but out of our own weakness and vulnerability. Just as the power of Christ comes from his surrender and death on the cross, so does the power of our life and witness come from our admission of weakness. We've nothing to offer God or our neighbor anything of our own doing or making.

As never before I'm gaining an understanding that as Jesus' disciples we're called to live a cruciform life, one that bears witness that we've entered the pattern of Christ's life, the pattern of the cross and resurrection. Jesus is reliving his life through us. We're filling up the full measure of his suffering and death, but we're also giving evidence to the power of the resurrection (Galatians 2:20; Colossians 1:24).

The Holy Spirit is at work drawing people to the Father the same way he drew them to himself when Jesus walked the earth. He draws them to the holy loving Savior who has always been the Christ of the cross. As the cross had its magnetic power when Jesus was lifted at Calvary, so the cross still draws people through the faithful lives and words of his followers (John 12:32). Only when we are clothed with the presence of Christ himself will the cynical culture around us give a hearing to the gospel of the cross, which to them first appears as foolish as was the gospel to the Jews and Gentiles of the first century.

I know that in my life and ministry sixteen years ago, it was necessary for me to experience an amount of cross bearing and death to self-will. This painful process of death to self-centered self is still going on in my old age. It's high time for me to surrender to and trust in Christ, believing that he will resurrect me in his time and in his own way, either in this life or the next. As God's people we must live the life of the cross and be armed with the message of the cross. It's a hard one for the unbelieving world to understand and accept, but it's also the only message that can change the world. We are entrusted with the message of the cross, which reveals God's wisdom and releases his powerful work. The cross of Christ is still our pattern for a life story worth telling. Some things never change!

# Run to Win!

## 1 Corinthians 9:19-27

> ¹⁹ *For though I am free with respect to all, I have made myself a slave to all, so that I might win more of them.* ²⁰ *To the Jews I became as a Jew, in order to win Jews. To those under the law I became as one under the law (though I myself am not under the law) so that I might win those under the law.* ²¹ *To those outside the law I became as one outside the law (though I am not free from God's law but am under Christ's law) so that I might win those outside the law.* ²² *To the weak I became weak, so that I might win the weak. I have become all things to all people, that I might by all means save some.* ²³ *I do it all for the sake of the gospel, so that I may share in its blessings.*
>
> ²⁴ *Do you not know that in a race the runners all compete, but only one receives the prize? Run in such a way that you may win it.* ²⁵ *Athletes exercise self-control in all things; they do it to receive a perishable wreath, but we an imperishable one.* ²⁶ *So I do not run aimlessly, nor do I box as though beating the air;* ²⁷ *but I punish my body and enslave it, so that after proclaiming to others I myself should not be disqualified.*

Paul employed images and illustrations from the world of sports, and the most popular sport of his day in Corinth was running, particularly in the bi-annual Isthmian Games, hosted by the city of Corinth, and second only to the Olympics in importance. You might say it was like the AFC vs. NFC game, leading up to the Super Bowl.

Paul makes it quite clear that the way God measures champions is not at all like the way the world measures them. In fact, not even like the way Christians sometimes measure champions. Paul was always being compared with those who called themselves "super apostles" (2 Cor. 11:5; 12:11), who claimed to have superior charismatic gifts, and more impressive public rhetoric and oratory. They were also, obviously, quite good at self-aggrandizement, and had convinced the people in the church that Paul, even though he had evangelized them, just didn't measure up to their standards for success. Paul describes his life and his God-given ministry as the running of a race, and his intention is to run to win.

In what seems like ancient history, I participated for 19 consecutive years in an annual mini-marathon, a 10-kilometer race. In community running events that often attract thousands of runners, there's an elite group who run to win, who finish in little more than half the time it takes participants like me. There's also a category that participates in the run as a fun social event.

To Paul, every believer has been enlisted to run a race of faith and faithful service, and we're to run to win! We're to be successful in God's sight by running life's race to please him, and are not in the race just for show, as were some of Paul's critics. So-called super apostles were influencing the church to measure success by the world's standards and not by God's. Christians today are also being duped by Satan and the fallen world into thinking they must measure up to their standards of what makes a person successful and important. To these false prophets, financial gain, and putting on an impressive display of intellect and oratory, and popularity with the world's people and worldly people in the church was all that mattered.

Paul's description of success God's way was a message needed by the church in the first century and by us as well. Paul says the Christian life is like a race. And our text essentially asks the question, "What are you running, i.e. living for?" And, "Are you running to succeed by God's standards?"

The race God has for us is run successfully, first, by winning people. People, to Paul, were a crown to be won. We live in a time and culture of self-centeredness. Just about everybody, and sometimes the church, as Paul would lament, is "looking out for number one." But if you want to run the race of life successfully God's way, your concerns must be with the infinite value of others, these precious souls God has placed in your daily "traffic patterns." Your spouse, and the children around your dinner table are those God has called you to win to faith. Your work associates, neighbors, and even your enemies are "fair game" to be won to

Christ though your prayers, your actions of loving concern, your willingness to forgive, and your godly example and seizing every opportunity to expose them to the good news of Jesus.

To win as many as possible, Paul was willing to renounce his personal rights and privileges (8:1-9:18). He accommodated himself to the conscience and need of others and was willing to relinquish his personal freedoms and legitimate indulgences for the sake of others. This is a challenge to us to become "world Christians," ready to relinquish our cultural preferences and prejudices to relate the gospel to people not like us, ethically, socially and politically. This willingness seems extraordinary in our American culture of individualism and self-aggrandizement. Yet, to be like the Savior, we must be willing to deny the self-centered self and follow the cross way of self-denial.

Some of us in the ministry profession can find ourselves accustomed to being given preferential treatment. Leaders run the risk of expecting special treatment. An airline flight attendant friend told me that among her colleagues, a certain well-known, (now retired, thankfully) television preacher has a horrible reputation for being rude, unreasonably demanding and downright obnoxious. He thinks he should be treated like a king, whereas Paul was content to be "the scum of the earth" for the sake of the gospel (1 Cor. 4:13). Paul endured all sorts of trials and abuse because his focus was not on his needs, rights, and privileges, but on the eternal prospects of people, and their urgent need for the gospel. Paul was not only willing, he was committed to doing whatever he could to eliminate artificial barriers that kept people from coming to faith in Christ.

All of us have unique contacts with people in our everyday life patterns. Some of these are family, old and new friends, and people we've yet to meet. Sometimes they're unlikely. A new friend I met at my former workout facility is a professional poker player and sports bar owner. Unlikely, you say, for a minister, yet we've become friends and he shares with me some of his and his family's needs. I pray for him and try to stay connected as a witness to him.

Paul says he's seeking also to win a prize (24-27). This athletic imagery was well received by the Corinthians, who were proud of their Isthmian Games. The crown awarded to the winners of these games was a wreath of celery worn on their heads! A far cry from a Winter Olympic gold medal or a Super Bowl ring! Probably thinking about the garland of celery leaves worn on the heads of their champions, Paul says we're running to win a prize that is of far greater worth than wilted vegetables! Paul speaks highly of the prize God gives to all who run the race of life his way.

It's not only permissible, but even commendable to seek after God's rewards. "Indeed, if we consider the unblushing promises of reward and the staggering nature of rewards promised in the Gospels, it would seem Our Lord finds our desires, not too strong, but too weak," says CS Lewis. He explains that rewards promised in Scripture are not mercenary and self-centered. For example, if the reward a man sought in marriage was a girl's inheritance, he would be venal. But to win a woman's love through marriage is the proper reward for his courtship. To fight in battle and risk one's life with deep patriotic love for one's country, and then be awarded and promoted in rank is not mercenary. It is the proper reward for service rendered (Lewis). We believers look for the rewards the Lord himself has promised us, for which he has given us a longing, the reward of pleasing God. The prize is to hear Jesus say, "Well done, you good and faithful servant" (Matt. 25:21), and to be finally and eternally like him in perfect love and character.

Paul knew he could not gain the prize, that he could not be God's champion, unless he went into strict training (25). The Isthmian games required strict training for 10 months, without which athletes would be declared ineligible. The athletes who compete in the Olympic Games or Super Bowl pay the price of years of rigorous training. They all seek to win medal, financial reward or recognition.

Paul was one who disciplined himself like a serious athlete, employing spiritual disciplines for growth in godliness. How much more do we need to avail ourselves of the disciplines upon which not only the apostle depended, but also our Lord Jesus depended, such as worship, prayer, the word, fasting, silence and solitude, evangelism, giving, learning, and perseverance. We grow and are made clean by abiding in Jesus, the True Vine (Jn. 15:1-17), and we grow by the way we respond to life's trials, which are God's way of disciplining us (Heb. 12:7-11). The athletes that will mount the awards platform will get there by strict discipline.

John Bunyan wrote his best and certainly most far-reaching work, *Pilgrim's Progress,* while in a Bedford jail. Similarly, Jonathan Edwards did his most significant writing after being fired from a long and fruitful pastorate in Northampton, and virtually exiled to an Indian settlement in the frontier village of Stockbridge in Western Massachusetts. God often sends his best servants through the fires of tribulation, to develop the discipline of perseverance that leads to maturity and godliness (Jas. 1:2-4).

In my long-ago past, I ran mini-marathons, just to remind myself to stay in decent shape. And there were times when, about a third of the way through the race, I gave serious thought to ducking out of the race, and walking through a wooded, secluded, obscure pathway, back to my car (or faking a leg cramp, or whatever).

Paul was fearful he would experience the disgrace of not finishing the race, of being disqualified as a spiritual leader (27). I know of too many ministers and active church members who dropped out of the race. Because of a moral or spiritual failure, they had to relinquish the prize for finishing the race. They'll go to heaven but have had to forfeit so much of the eternal reward, that which comes to those who finish well, who are faithful to the end, and whose lives cause no embarrassment to the Kingdom.

Everyone can run successfully. Some are during the pursuit of your career and perhaps are wondering if your life can have any significance. You may have been told by your boss you're a failure in business, or Satan may be telling you you've failed as a spouse or parent or that you're a failure in life itself. I'm here to tell you, on the authority of God's word that you can be successful in God's eyes because of his grace through Jesus Christ.

Paul spoke of seeking to reach the goal and win the game for which Jesus Christ had captured and enlisted him. Christ enlists and then he enables us to run successfully (Phil. 3:12). To run to win, all you need is the grace of God, given when we follow Jesus as Lord. Immediately he puts you into the race of your life! He also takes us believers who might have grown weary and even dropped out of the race, and he lifts us and encourages us to resume running.

In most races and games, there's only one winner. In God's race, he gives the prize to all who finish the race. That's what Paul told Timothy he had done, at the close of his life: "I have finished the race" (2 Tim. 4:7). Maybe you haven't thought well of yourself and have been an underachiever in the race of faith. But God thinks highly of you and cheers you on as a winner. I was impressed to see a runner stop before the finish line and lift and help carry a fallen runner to the finish line. There are some fallen runners you and I can help.

Kent Hughes told the story of Bill Broadhurst, who in 1981 entered the Pepsi Challenge 10,000-meter race in Omaha, Nebraska. "Surgery ten years earlier for a brain aneurysm had left him paralyzed on his left side. Now, on that misty July morning, he stands with 1,200 lithe men and women at the starting line.

"The gun sounds! The crowd surges forward. Bill throws his stiff left leg forward, pivots on it as his foot hits the ground. His slow plop-plop-plop rhythm seems to mock him as the pack races into the distance. Sweat rolls down his face, pain pierces his ankle, but he keeps going. Some of the runners complete the race in about 30 minutes, but 2 hours and 29 minutes later Bill reaches the finish line. A man approaches from a small group of remaining bystanders. Though exhausted, Bill recognizes him from pictures in the newspaper. He is Bill Rodgers, the famous marathon runner, who then drapes his newly won medal around Bill's neck. Bill Broadhurst's finish was as glorious as that of the world's greatest----though he finished last. Why? Because he ran with perseverance" (Hughes, 160f).

Let's stay in the race!

# How We Grieve

## 1 Thessalonians 4:13-18

> *¹³ But we do not want you to be uninformed, brothers and sisters, about those who have died, so that you may not grieve as others do who have no hope. ¹⁴ For since we believe that Jesus died and rose again, even so, through Jesus, God will bring with him those who have died. ¹⁵ For this we declare to you by the word of the Lord, that we who are alive, who are left until the coming of the Lord, will by no means precede those who have died. ¹⁶ For the Lord himself, with a cry of command, with the archangel's call and with the sound of God's trumpet, will descend from heaven, and the dead in Christ will rise first. ¹⁷ Then we who are alive, who are left, will be caught up in the clouds together with them to meet the Lord in the air; and so we will be with the Lord forever. ¹⁸ Therefore encourage one another with these words.*

There's an old gospel song by Jeremiah Rankin titled *Tell It to Jesus*, with a fourth verse that asks this question that could well have been asked of the church at Thessalonica:

> *Are you troubled at the thought of dying?*
> *Tell it to Jesus, tell it to Jesus;*
> *For Christ's coming Kingdom are you sighing?*
> *Tell it to Jesus alone.*

Church historian Martin Marty says that a strong majority of Americans share a belief in eternal life, and yet they live in terror of death. For many, their belief in everlasting life is founded on wishful thinking rather than on a personal and biblical faith. It is for them a false security. I sensed the irony of the theme of death during the Halloween season, when death becomes a fantasy world reserved for goblins, zombies and ghosts, whose task is to scare us in haunted houses on Trick or Treat Night. We don't really think about the reality of death.

For the believers in Thessalonica, and perhaps for some here today, there's a fear of death because of a misunderstanding of the promises and truths of God's word. Some of you perhaps have a legitimate fear of death because you're unsure of a life-changing, eternal-life giving relationship with Christ. Paul says affectionately yet straightforwardly, "Brothers and sisters, we don't want you to be uninformed about these matters."

Perhaps you were a *Peanuts* fan, and in one of Charles Schultz's cartoons, Lucy looks out of a window and wonders, "Boy, look at it rain! What if it floods the whole world?" "It will never do that," answers Linus. "In the ninth chapter of Genesis, God promised Noah that would never happen again, and the sign of that promise is the rainbow." "You've taken a great load off of my mind," replies Lucy, to which Linus responds, "Sound theology has a way of doing that."

Paul hopes to take a load off the troubled minds of believers, who were burying their Christian family and friends. Evidently there were believers in a bit of turmoil over the fact of death, which was facing them day after day. Would these departed ones miss out on the return of Christ, which they thought was imminent?

The general climate of the ancient world was one of gloom, even though the Greek Gnostics had a quasi-hope of the immortality of the soul. Most believed that death was simply the end, as did many of the Jews.

FF Bruce quotes a 2nd century letter of condolence written from one friend to another:

"I sorrowed and wept over your dear departed one, as I wept over Didymas…but really, there is nothing I can do in the face of such things. So please comfort each other."

Paul was writing to remind them of hope, as an important part of the faith-hope-love triad that runs throughout the Thessalonian letters. Just as we are to please God by growing in holiness by faith, and by growing in love for one another, so are we to grow in hope for life everlasting, for ourselves and for our fellow believers.

In our passage of Scripture, Paul seems to be saying two truths that are vital for our understanding of biblical hope. Paul's statement in verse 13 implies the reality of grief. The Bible notes the sorrow over death as a normal human emotion. Ecclesiastes notes that God has "set eternity in the hearts of men;" (3:11), so it is normal to think of death as unnatural and certainly unwelcome.

Death comes as an abrupt intruder to life, a tragedy, which is not a biblical word, but is rather a pagan Greek word, attributed to a culture that didn't know a sovereign God, but was rather subject to the whims and fates of lesser gods and fate.

Following the tragedy of the horrendous mass shooting in a small Texas town last Sunday, our nation is faced once again with the uncertainty of life and the possibility of death. These massacres are happening with such frequency one news report said that America is no longer shocked by but are becoming numb to tragedy.

And as a congregation, we're grieving the loss of one of our long-time, faithful members. We grieve her loss, even though we are grateful for her long life and confident of our hope that she's with the Lord. Even Jesus understood and shared the emotion of sadness and sorrow over separation caused by death. He wept at the tomb of his friend Lazarus (Jn. 11:35).

Leighton Ford, Presbyterian minister and former associate evangelist with Billy Graham, shared his grief experience over the death of his 21-year-old son, Sandy. He noted that our struggle in such a time of grief is in bringing our faith and emotions together. We have common human emotions, but by the grace of God we can bring our faith to bear upon them, but there is a struggle to do so. Death takes our loved one from us into the realm of the unknown, and to a place where we cannot go. It's the separation of a long journey.

You know the sadness of saying good-bye to your spouse and family when you leave for a long visit or move to another state or country. Death for the believer brings the sad emotion of saying "good-bye" to a loved-one. It may be that in the eyes of the world the death is a real tragedy. Leighton Ford said in retrospect, "Yes, I believe God is good and strong and that he brings blessing out of pain. But I would be less than honest if I didn't acknowledge the part of me inside that says, 'It's not right'" (177).

And so, we grieve, but do so with a difference. *The Message* paraphrases verse 13, "First off, you must not carry on over them like people who have nothing to look forward to, as if the grave were the last word." We grieve, says Paul, but with a hope for the life to come. This hope that makes all the difference is based on Jesus' death and resurrection. Paul gives this most foundational confession of faith: *"For since we believe that Jesus died and rose again, even so, through Jesus, God will bring with him those who have died"* (14).

When Paul speaks of the death of a believer, he uses different words and terminology, like "to sleep." Paul doesn't say that Jesus slept, but that he died. He suffered the full experience of death as the consequence of sin. Not his sin, but ours. He suffered death as the curse for our sin and was separated from the Father during his hours of God-forsaken-ness on the cross.

Because of Christ's death, the grave has been robbed of its victory (1Cor. 15: 55-57). We now can call our experience being asleep in Jesus. But the empty philosophy of our age has a wishful thinking *ersatz* hope called reincarnation. Many who deny Jesus' resurrection look to him as a good moral example and not as a risen Savior. Ed Steimle said that the older he gets, the less he gets out of good moral principles and noble examples. He wants a Savior who can give power to change life, and victory over death. We need a life-over-death deliverer!

In recent years there has been a pseudo-scientific effort to assuage our fears of death, with people like Raymond Moody and Elizabeth Kubler-Ross, and their theories of thanatology. These psychologists and physicians try to prove the existence of life after death based on the testimonials of folks who purportedly died and returned to tell us about it. But our hope is not based on such empty theories, but on the word of God. Paul's triad in 1Thessalonians is faith, hope and love. Without a real hope our faith is meaningless, and love is just sentimentality (1 Cor.15: 12-19. If there's no resurrection for us, there wasn't any for Jesus, and so this whole Christianity thing is a big hoax.

Death for the believer is so different Scripture uses the analogy of sleep. In our NRSV text, the Greek is not the word "death" but the expression "fallen asleep." Sleep, unlike death, is harmless, healthy and temporary. Jesus spoke of Lazarus, who was dead, as being asleep (Jn. 11:11). Paul spoke of his preference for being absent from the body, which sleeps in death, and being present with the Lord (Phil. 1:23; 2 Cor. 5:8).

The word for cemetery means "place of sleep" (koimterion). Our bodies, though decaying, are in the mind of God as asleep in Jesus. When Jesus returns, and here it's clearly not a secret rapture, He'll come with all who've gone ahead to be with the Lord. Then, the bodies of believers will be raised to meet the Lord, and all who remain with alive bodies, will also be caught up to meet the Lord.

Death doesn't separate us, but rather unites us with the Lord (Rom. 8:38f), and Jesus told the thief on the cross that he would be with him that day in Paradise (Lk. 23:43). This is clearly not what some call soul-sleep, that is, loss of consciousness. This is the temporary sleep of the body during a time of being disembodied, but present with the Lord in a glorious estate in heaven.

Warren Wiersbe tells of a friend whose wife died. He was approached by a friend, who said, "I'm sorry you lost your wife." "I didn't lose her, because you haven't lost anything if you know where it is, and I know where she is."

What glory for those who have gone to be with Jesus! We grieve the separation, but we certainly don't sorrow for them.

CS Lewis, in *A Grief Observed*, said he finally, as he worked through the long grief process of losing his wife Joy, came to the point of realizing that even if he could bring her back to life with him, it wouldn't be fair to her.

There's a partial reunion going on in heaven all the time, as believers are reunited in heaven. But Paul tells of the great reunion when Jesus returns, when he will come triumphantly as the King of kings. This verb translated "to meet" was used to describe the action of dignitaries in a city, going out to the city gate to meet an arriving hero, perhaps a victorious king. And then the king and the accompanying dignitaries would enter the city together.

Leighton Ford said he and his wife, Jeannie, grieved over the death of their beautiful, bright, athletic, and talented son, Sandy, but he says theirs was "a clean grief." It was not sullied by regrets, and by anger with God. Even though they questioned God, they waited long enough to learn to trust him, and to be reassured of his love. They came to believe in the purposes of God, who was glorified in Sandy's life, and that his potential is being fulfilled in heaven.

CH Spurgeon said that the Greek word in verse 17 is *sun* and not *meta*. We will not just be alongside the Lord in heaven but will be *in him* completely. This means we'll be perfectly righteous and holy and loving, just as he is. This means all our human potential will be fulfilled, and we'll be more glorious than Adam and Eve before the fall.

Paul gave the church not a lesson in theology just to satisfy their curiosity, but so they would have truth to share with those experiencing grief. How blessed I am by the way this church minister to one another in times of grief! CH Spurgeon once again said that funeral services ought to include congregational hymns of praise. Funerals ought to be also services of celebrating everlasting life.

We grieve, Paul said, but not like the hopeless. Being in an airport is a reminder of the mixture of tears of sadness with departure and joy upon reunion. You see couples and families embracing with tears of "good-bye," as a loved one departs for a long journey. But then you see tears of joy as long-departed loved ones are welcomed home.

A piece of doggerel, which was an epitaph, appeared on a tombstone in an old British cemetery:

*Pause, my friend, as you walk by;*
*As you are now, so once was I.*
*As I am now, so you will be.*
*Prepare, my friend, to follow me!*

A visitor scratched this reply,

*To follow you is not my intent,*
*Until I know which way you went.* (Wiersbe)

We know which way all of departed God's children went. They went to be with Jesus. One of the last things my wife Nancy said to me before she lost consciousness was, tearfully, "I want to be with Jesus." I know which way she went.

We need to affirm our faith in the risen Christ, who will overcome our fear of death because he has already given us victory over death. All who want to be with Jesus now will be with him for eternity. Our hope is in being with Jesus and all who have known him and gone before us into his glorious presence.

# Resurrection Children of God

## 1 John 2:28-3:3

> *²⁸And now, little children, abide in him, so that when he is revealed we may have confidence and not be put to shame before him at his coming. ²⁹ If you know that he is righteous, you may be sure that everyone who does right has been born of him. 3 ¹ See what love the Father has given us, that we should be called children of God; and that is what we are. The reason the world does not know us is that it did not know him. ² Beloved, we are God's children now; what we will be has not yet been revealed. What we do know is this: when he is revealed, we will be like him, for we will see him as he is. ³ And all who have this hope in him purify themselves, just as he is pure.*

The second coming of Christ is a major theme in Scripture, appearing 318 times in the 260 chapters of the New Testament. And always Christ's return is a practical doctrine, an incentive for godly, faithful living, and never as a matter for satisfying curiosity or providing material for prophecy preachers who give sermons and write books about their speculations and predictions.

The church has been in the "last days" since the risen Christ ascended to heaven and poured out the Spirit on the church at Pentecost to equip us for living the Great Commandment (Mk. 12:28-34) and doing the Great Commission (Matt. 28:19-20). And each generation is to live in readiness for Christ's return, which is certainly closer than it's ever been! But our readiness doesn't come from trying to speculate and satisfy our curiosity, but in living with hope that motivates us to purity of life and perseverance in service. As someone has said, "The best way to prepare for the last days is to focus on the first things!"

As resurrection children of God, we live with a hope in Christ's return. John uses that tender address, "dear children," reminding them that in a way they are his spiritual children, but more importantly are the beloved children of God. As God's children they have a duty to the heavenly Father. Sometimes we think of duty as an onerous, burdensome task, like doing excessive homework for an overly demanding, unreasonable school teacher or extra work from an employer who requires all our "free" time. But Webster's first definition of duty is "respect." But it's not about being dutiful but about abiding in Christ in a faithful love relationship, characterized by staying in the Word and seeking intimate fellowship with him, and living in step with the Holy Spirit.

We must abide in Christ in order to be able to stand before him with confidence when he returns. One scholar calls this a "balanced eschatology," which calls us to remain in Christ *now* so we can stand before him *then* (Smalley). This word "confidence" (*parresia*) we are to have in the presence of the returning Christ is also "fearlessness and joyousness" (Yarbrough). As we abide with Christ in an intimate love relationship of trust, dependence and obedience, we can stand before him as a much-loved, uninhibited child, excitedly greeting a returning parent!

Most of us can probably remember *at least one experience* in childhood or in our teen years when we did our duty to our parents and were unashamed (2:28) when they returned home to examine our work. We were confident they would be pleased because we didn't disappoint them, and we were confident of their appreciation as loving parents.

The confidence of the abiding, obedient child is contrasted with the embarrassment and shame of the disobedient. John implies that false teachers will be the ones ashamed before Christ when he appears. But all followers of Christ will meet him with unashamed confidence and joyful assurance, having been justified through faith in him (Rom. 5:1f). Of course, we'll all stand before the judgment seat of Christ and give an accounting before him and receive rewards based upon the faithful stewardship of our lives (Rom. 14:10; 2 Cor. 5:10; Matt. 25:14-30). But all of God's believing, resurrection children, will be greeted by the loving, waiting Father (Lk. 15: 11-32).

Our duty, however, is to live a righteous life that is evidence of a genuine rebirth. "If you know that he is righteous, you know that everyone who does what is right has been born of him" (2:29). The *New Living Translation* says, "Since we know that Christ is righteous, we also know that all who do what is right are God's children," God's resurrection children. Right conduct is not a condition for rebirth but a consequence of it.

The thought that we have been created and are being recreated as God's beloved children should produce "an outburst of wonder" (Stott, 3:1). This sense of the "wonder of it all" arrests John as he writes: "'Look!' he says, 'Look at the love the Father has given us. We are called children of God. And we are!'" (Morris). I'm afraid we have lost, or worse, have never contemplated this glorious truth and privilege, to be claimed and even loved by the heavenly Father as his resurrection children. And he loves us as only he can, with a lavish love beyond our comprehension.

Nothing disturbs us more than reports of abused or neglected children. John addressed this letter to the church during a Greco-Roman culture that was often cruel and inhumane in the treatment of children. Fathers were free to dispose of unwanted babies, who were often "left to die in an out of the way place." What a precious thought this was to John's readers, and should be also to us, that we are God's beloved children, whom he's begotten and adopted as objects of his love and delight.

This is what Calvin calls "the dignity and excellence of our calling" as God's children. We're not only named as God's children but have been chosen to be his children before the creation (Eph. 1:4). God sent his Son to redeem us in order that he might adopt us with the full privileges of his children. And he gave us the Spirit who prompts us to call upon God as our "Abba Father," our dear heavenly Father (Gal. 4:4-7). God's great love is the reason we've been given the privilege of being his children. The price he paid for our being his children is the cross of Jesus, his beloved eternal Son (1 Pet. 1:18f).

To be called God's resurrection children is to accept the challenge of our identification with Christ (3:1). We're God's children, "unknown" and often misunderstood in this dark, unbelieving and Christ-rejecting world. We can expect to be misunderstood and spurned by others, as was Jesus (3:1 and Jn. 1:10f). To be a child of God is to face the challenge of being misunderstood and rejected by the unconverted, lost world around us, whether in the home, classroom, workplace or communities where we live. Resurrection children share in Christ's sufferings, the way of self-denial, sacrificial service, and forgiving love for our enemies (Matt. 16:24ff; Col. 1:24; Matt. 5:43-48).

Those who suffer persecution as Christ followers have the blessing of unmistakable assurance of being the children of God (Matt. 5:10). Regardless of how cruel and demeaning their persecution, those who suffer for Christ have a dignity that the world cannot take away or even diminish. And the hostile world doesn't realize who they are "messing with"—the anointed of God (Ps. 105:15). These persecutors certainly will face Christ with shame.

The story is told that during slavery days in America, "some northern visitors in New Orleans were watching a company of slaves wearily shuffling along the dock, returning to their work. Spiritless, apparently indifferent to life itself, they were dragging themselves along. But one, in striking contrast, with head erect and with unbroken spirit, strode among them with the dignified bearing of a conqueror. 'Who is that fellow?' someone asked. 'Is he the *straw boss*; or the owner of the slaves?' 'No,' was the answer; 'that fellow just can't get it out of his head that he is the son of a king.' And so, he was. He had been dragged into slavery as a small child, but he had already been taught that he was no ordinary person; he was the son of a king, and must bear himself accordingly, if he lives. Now, after half a lifetime of hardship and abuse, which had broken the spirit of others, he was still the son of a king! Such," says the writer, "is the inspiration and the strength of the (children) of God!" (Koller).

The promises that the believer is destined to be like Jesus when we see him in his unveiled glory is "probably the highest 'shouting ground' for believers" in the entire Bible (Koller on 3:2). Paul also says that "When Christ, who is your life, appears, then you will also appear with him in glory" (Col. 3:4).

The Apostle Paul also puts this hope in the context of God's sovereign purpose for our lives when he says, *"We know that all things work together for good for those who love God, who are called according to his purpose. For those whom he foreknew he also predestined to be conformed to the image of his Son, in order that he might be the firstborn within a large family. And those whom he predestined he also called; and those whom he called he also justified; and those whom he justified he also glorified."* (Rom. 8:28-30). God is at work in our lives, in all the twists and turns and even those that bewilder us, to prepare us for everlasting glory.

In our present condition, even as the redeemed children of God, we can't look on the fullness of God's glory. Moses was denied seeing God's full glory. The Lord told him "you cannot see my face, for no one may see me and live" (Ex. 33:18-20). David evidently hoped for the sight of seeing God's face when he wrote,

"And I—in righteousness I shall see your face; when I awake, I shall be satisfied with seeing your likeness" (Ps. 17:15).

What was denied to Moses and longed for by David will be granted to all the resurrection children of God when Jesus comes or when we go to be with him in the glory of his presence in Paradise. The reason we may behold him in all his glory is that all sin will be removed from us and we will undergo the transformation of becoming perfectly like Jesus in godliness.

I have a lot of questions about how to prepare to meet Christ and the mysteries of the future life, but I simply need to trust God with the unknown, as Paul says: "Now we see but a poor reflection as in a mirror; then we shall see face to face. Now I know in part; then I shall know fully, even as I am fully known" (1 Cor. 13:12). As God's resurrection children we have now what is a mysterious but will certainly be a glorious destiny. We don't know what we *shall* be, but we know what we *should* be.

This hope of sharing the glory of Christ is the very heart of the New Testament teaching about everlasting rewards. As CS Lewis said, the Gospels are replete with "the unblushing promises of reward" of a "staggering nature," and we God's people should deeply desire those rewards. "We should not be troubled by unbelievers when they say that this promise of reward makes the Christian life a mercenary affair. There are different kinds of reward. There is the reward which has no connection with the things you do to earn it, and quite foreign to the desires that ought to accompany those things. Money is not the natural reward of love; that is why we call a man mercenary if he marries a woman for the sake of her money. But marriage is the proper reward for a real lover, and he is not mercenary for desiring it."

Our hope is for the fulfillment of all that Christ has begun in us to make us like himself. When we become like Jesus we'll discover the unspeakably glorious and delightful eternity he had in mind for us at the beginning. When we see Jesus and become like him that will be reward enough and will open to us an eternity of pleasures at his "right hand" (Ps. 16:11).

God's resurrection children who are being purified by hope and long for his appearing (2 Tim. 4:8) are also the ones who make the most impact on this world, whether through being the quiet leaven of a godly character, being mighty in intercessory prayer, or taking a stand for social reform. Think of women like Teresa of Calcutta and men like William Wilberforce. "Lord Shaftesbury (1801-1885), the great English social reformer and a mature Christian, said near the end of his life, 'I do not think that in the last forty years I have ever lived one conscious hour that was not influenced by the thought of our Lord's return" (Boice).

And so, we live in the awareness of seeing Jesus and receiving his everlasting benediction, when we hope to hear him say, "Well done, good and faithful servant! You have been faithful with a few things; I will put you in charge of many things. Come and share your master's happiness!" (Matt. 25:21).

Being purified by hope might be likened to someone expecting a large financial gift which, as promised, is being sent in the mail. With "expectant assurance," the beneficiary lays plan to spend the money. "Its arrival, after all, is just a matter of time" (Yarbrough). Our hope is even more certain. We should begin living like God's resurrection children who will be free from all sin, will become like

Jesus, and thus will be more than compensated for anything we give or spend for Jesus.

The Second Coming of Christ *is* a practical doctrine and should make a difference in the way you and I live today. We don't know when Jesus will return to earth, but it's certain, that if he doesn't in your or my lifetime we'll certainly go to meet him and stand before him. May none of us be ashamed and unprepared when he returns or when we depart to be with him; but may we all be able to stand before him joyfully as the redeemed resurrection children of God!

www.ingramcontent.com/pod-product-compliance
Lightning Source LLC
Chambersburg PA
CBHW052140110526
44591CB00012B/1793